Let's Face It

Let's Face It

WRITING AND ARTWORK FROM PARC

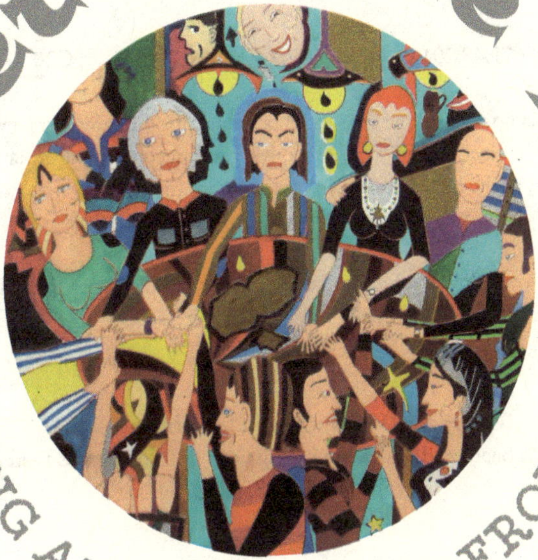

Edited by Hume Cronyn & Chris Beyers

mosaic press

Library and Archives Canada Cataloguing in Publication

Let's face it : writings and artwork from PARC / Hume Cronyn and Chris Beyers.

ISBN 978-0-88962-931-8

1. Canadian poetry (English)--Ontario--Toronto. 2. Canadian poetry (English)--21st century. 3. Art, Canadian--Ontario--Toronto--21st century. I. Cronyn, Hume, 1957- II. Beyers, Chris, 1961- III. Parkdale Activity Recreation Centre

PS8295.7.T67L48 2011 C811'.60809207409713541 C2011-901283-9

Published by Mosaic Press, offices and warehouse at 1252 Speers Road, Units 1 and 2, Oakville, Ontario, L6L 5N9, Canada and Mosaic Press, 40 Sonwil Dr, Cheektowaga, NY14225, U.S.A.

ISBN 978-0-88962-931-8

We acknowledge the financial support of the Government of Canada through the Canada Book Fund (CBF) for this project.

Nous reconnaissons l'aide financière du gouvernement du Canada par l'entremise du Fonds du livre du Canada (FLC) pour ce projet.

Canadian Heritage Patrimoine canadien

Canada

Mosaic Press in Canada:
1252 Speers Road, Units 1 & 2
Oakville, Ontario
L6L 5N9
Phone/Fax: 905-825-2130
info@mosaic-press.com

Mosaic Press in U.S.A.:
c/o Livingston, 40 Sonwil Dr,
Cheektowaga, NY
14225
Phone/Fax: 905-825-2130
info@mosaic-press.com

www.mosaic-press.com

We look down, but we don't see the earth,
we look up but we don't see the sky...

what will the gods do with us? ...

1 Dec. 2011

- Elias Tabar

To brother Ted
with best wishes
from Elias
Merry X-mas

Thanks

Table of Contents

THE STRUGGLE FOR MENTAL HEALTH

BEING IGNORED / ESTRANGED

SOCIAL JUSTICE

THE LIGHTER SIDE

SECRET PLACES: SAFE PLACES

NATURE'S SOLACE

with artwork by:

Branko Aleksic
David Morriseau
Derrick Harwin
Don Baker
Elias Tabar
James Smith
Martin Owen
Mike Knox
Renata Edan
Tyde

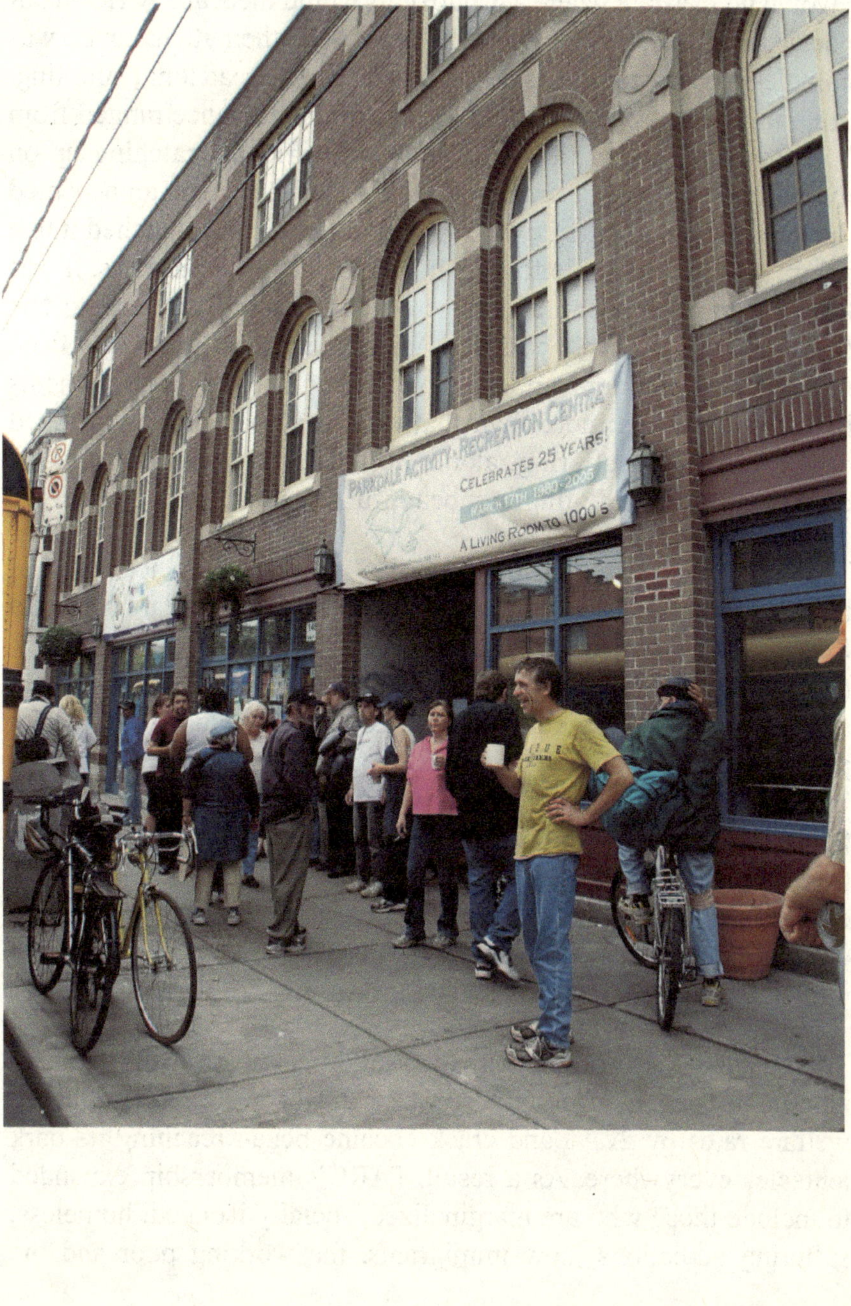
PARKDALE ACTIVITY - RECREATION
CELEBRATES 25 YEARS!
MARCH 17TH 1980-2005
A LIVING ROOM TO 1000'S

Introduction

I can remember years ago, when I began writing, every Monday night I would go to a café where a group of us would meet and perform our poetry in the basement. One of the poets, a mathematician, who was homeless and in precarious mental health, would read long, rambling, often incoherent poems. The response of the audience ranged from boredom, to nodding off, to chatting with friends, catching up on the past week. For six months this persisted—became an accepted fact in a usually exciting evening—but one night he launched into a poem, his usual mumble forged into a resolute articulateness. It was the most moving poem, about the death of his mother, and no one fidgeted, or fell asleep, or chatted. We were all ears. Seemingly from nowhere, this poem of unbelievable feeling sprung. Few moments have impacted me more than that one. A person can be stripped down, burdened, suffering, alone, buffeted, but given a chance to create, the most spine-tingling, beautiful poem can spring forth.

This book is the product of the PARC writing workshop and has been in the making for the past ten years. PARC (Parkdale Activity-Recreation Centre) was founded in 1980 by concerned citizens in the Parkdale neighbourhood and the Ministry of Health. It was a response to a governmental policy of de-institutionalization, where psychiatric patients were discharged from hospitals and released into the community. The problem was that the policy, a humane one, floundered because there was a lack of supports in the community to effect the much vaunted ideal of reintegration. PARC was established to be one of those supports, a community centre that offered a safe haven from the harsh realities of the street and the intolerable conditions of substandard boarding houses.

Two events in the mid-nineties had a shattering impact on the Parkdale community. The conservative government of Mike Harris slashed welfare rates by 22 % and crack cocaine began reaching its dark tentacles everywhere. As a result, PARC's membership expanded to include those who are marginalized, socially isolated, homeless, suffering addictions, new immigrants, the working poor and the poverty-stricken. The needs of this disparate group of people are overwhelming and, at times when these needs compete for limited resources, PARC is stretched to its absolute limits. But despite these hardships, it is rather amazing how these different constituents, abetted by the spirit of tolerance and co-operation, come together and make for an unusually complex and vital community.

PARC offers a range of services. Fundamental is basic human sustenance and shelter. PARC serves two meals a day, seven days a week. In addition to being a housing advocate, it helps members find places, supports people with serious mental health and addiction problems to keep their housing, and in 2000 it became a housing provider. Although PARC spends a great deal of time wrestling with the socio-economic forces of poverty that overwhelm most of our members, it is mindful of the hunger that our members have for intellectual, emotional and spiritual nourishment. As one of the members so succinctly stated, "I appreciate that PARC feeds me when I can't make ends meet, but, more important, I come to PARC for spiritual sustenance." PARC is at its best when there is a raft of programs where members are encouraged to learn, engage in a host of physical activities, creatively express themselves, have access to job training and job opportunities, or sit on the board of directors and a variety of committees. The writing workshop is one of these programs and has been meeting weekly for the past twenty-five years.

In the past ten years, the workshop has taken place in three different rooms, somewhat mirroring the changes in PARC. During that time, PARC has undergone major renovations, expanding from a dingy, smoke-filled drop-in room to a building that offers ten housing units, an outreach program, job creation, and a more spacious drop-in area. The first room we used – before PARC undertook renovations – was in the old food bank, a deserted storefront room with nothing but an odd assortment of fold-up tables and beat-up chairs. This was a period when the group was most dynamic, averaging twelve to fifteen writers every Thursday workshop. The energy was electric. There was a distinct feeling that this was the highlight of everyone's week. Our standard format was to write for twenty minutes, and then go around the table and read out our efforts. The sessions would range from exercises concentrating on observation and description, to exploratory ones such as writing down dreams and automatic writing, to playful ones such as starting from a random word chosen from the dictionary, or pretending to be an object, a season, etc, to thematic exercises such as the happiest, most illuminating, or most challenging moments in one's life. Several times I was amazed how the same image would pop up in four different pieces, as if we were plugged into some telepathic energy with a direct link to the collective unconscious. We're seven years past those halcyon days, but still the memory of that energy brings a smile to my face.

During the period when PARC was undergoing renovations, the writing workshop was moved to a storage cupboard on the second floor. This was a zany time when we wrote surrounded by hockey bags of unwashed and pungent-smelling equipment, a cardboard box brimming with bathing suits, several vases sprouting bouquets of paint brushes, even a wooden toilet seat. One small window let in natural light, and on dark days an antique floor lamp that continually shorted provided sporadic light. Sometimes, adversity and quirkiness of setting can feed the creative juices, and again this was a productive period for the writing workshop.

With the renovations completed, the writing workshop moved to our new space on the second floor, the Edmond Yu room with its pumpkin orange walls, its cherry red floor and its forest green chairs. Edmond Yu was a PARC member who was tragically gunned down by the police. The room is graced with a bank of windows overlooking the hustle and bustle of Queen Street. The past year has been a low point in the life of the workshop, perhaps somewhat stalled by the frustrated expectation relating to the long-overdue publication of this book. I feel that there is an overwhelming need to bring our work to a point of completion – in this case a published book – before we can move onto our next stage.

Over the years writers have come and gone and we have made an effort to represent as many of them as possible. PARC's first book, *Kiss Me You Mad Fool*, published in 1990, only presented writers from the writing workshop. In contrast, *Let's Face It* has cast a larger net and includes a wider sampling of writers from the entire PARC community. For example, there's a number of writers who don't come to the writing workshop, but faithfully attend the monthly Poetry Nite. Then there's Guy Ewing who works at Project Read, a literacy program in Parkdale. He attended a Poetry Nite several years ago and became a regular. When Jo Petite, who facilitates the literacy program at PARC went on maternity leave, Guy filled in for her, and for several years continued to facilitate the group. It's this lovely sense of entanglement that deepens community &, in our view, argues for the inclusion of his writing. One of the unique things about the workshop is that a number of staff, plus college students who've had year-long placements at PARC, have helped facilitate the group and some of their writing has also been included. Finally, Renata's son, Anton, and my daughter, Chloe, attended some workshops over Easter break when they were twelve and we were unable to find babysitters. Both their pieces are found in "The Lighter Side" section.

In *Kiss Me You Mad Fool*, the writings were organized in sections by author, thus showcasing the individual's creativity. This book is organized differently. To furnish the context for the rest of the book, the first two sections consist of pieces about PARC and the writing workshop. Thereafter the book is organized by themes such as *The Struggle for Mental Health, Social Justice, The Lighter Side, Nature's Solace*, etc. The hope is to evoke something of the multiform character of the PARC community – a creative expression of our journey through pain, despair, hope, joy, friendship, struggle. The final section of the book closes with a photo and autobiography of each of the writers and artists. We also have included the paintings of various artists at PARC. Right from the beginning, when we first conceptualized the book, we considered that the paintings needed to be an integral part of it, as examples of PARC's bustling creativity. There's one painting I want to comment on: David Morriseau's painting in the first section. The painting is a 4 x 8 foot mural portraying the members of the Imperial Breakfast Club. The Imperial Breakfast Club (named after the sherry) is a harm reduction group at PARC that has been meeting since 2007. The mural is the product of the collective effort of the club; it was designed and directed by David, who guided his friends in painting the initial layers, before completing the painting by adding the black lines and details.

Recently, there has been a spate of deaths at PARC, one of them being Bobbi, a writer in this book and mainstay of Poetry Nite. When Bobbi first came to Poetry Nite, she would read in-your-face erotic verse that unsettled her audience, but as she continued coming she broadened out, reading poems from Robert Frost, Chrystos, and, her favorite, Marge Piercy. She then emceed several Poetry Nites, began writing again, and joined the writing workshop. One afternoon, she claimed that she wanted to write a piece about alienation. She went home, and returning next day said that she couldn't write about alienation but that she'd written another piece. That piece was 'Jigsaw' and it begins the book. Often she wondered how her writing could tap into her pain without being melodramatic.

When Bobbi died, she lay in her apartment room several days before she was discovered. A week after her death I was sitting around the table with four others. Michael was relating how he lived directly below Bobbi by seven floors – the layout of his apartment identical to Bobbi's – and that like her he lived on his own, had few visitors and had a pet cat. Then he mentioned that he could die under similar circumstances. The other three people at the table acknowledged that this could happen to them too – no melodrama, just the dense weight of fact. In a burst of feeling, Michael then noted the abundance of talent and creativity that there is at PARC and how much of it remains untapped. He could not understand a society that allowed so much talent to go to waste. In my view this book is an eloquent testimony against such a society.

—Hume Cronyn

A comment on editing this book

Editing a book such as this requires having some underlying concept that defines what kinds of elements should be included, and how these should be organized and presented. This concept is 'community', to the extent that we assumed at first that readers would consist mainly of people within the broader PARC community. As we put the book together, we saw that there may be a larger audience; nonetheless, PARC's ideals and activities, which bring together people from various walks of life, are very much at the heart of the conception of the book.

The writers are only to some extent representative of the broader PARC 'community', for there are many others at PARC who were not drawn to the writing workshop and to contributing to this project. As to what 'community' consists of at PARC, there are differing viewpoints. Is PARC first of all a 'thick', face-to-face community, where friendships and relations of mutual care and support can be cultivated over time; a place characterized by dense interweaving of stories based on more or less common experiences and memories; and where an individual's roles and standing in community is defined by who he or she is for others? Or is it rather a somewhat 'thin' community dedicated to ensuring that individual members' rights are protected; to providing for their basic needs as well as maximizing care services and fairly distributing them in an accountable manner; and to putting in place certain rules and procedures for respecting interpersonal and organizational boundaries? Is PARC a 'home' in the world, a place of belonging where people are recognized as full human beings and moral equals, having been denied this elsewhere; or is it essentially a place that provides food, clothing, and a temporary reprieve from the cold, and from exposure to the outside world? The answer is probably all of the above.

Our approach was to engender an occasion that would allow the authors to speak to such questions in their own unique ways. To be sure, many who have attended the writing workshop have tended to have a 'thicker' involvement in PARC activities. The PARC revealed by this work is a place in the city where people come together by bringing their experiences, including of profound loneliness and alienation, into contact with one another. It takes courage, and some measure of hope, to do this in a public domain.

Criteria for the selection of pieces were as follows: First, we wanted to ensure that the works of all workshop regulars were included. Second, we considered what people associated with PARC thought was interesting, truthful, and relevant to their experiences. Thus, for example, we took into account comments made by writers in the workshop on one another's pieces, feedback by other PARC members and staff, and so on. Finally, at times we also considered what the value of a piece was for its author, and what it might mean for him or her to have it published.

Once we had collected a pool of writings, we came up with a series of categories that most of the pieces seemed to fit. The compilation process consisted of continually collecting and incorporating new pieces over the years, modifying and redefining the categories accordingly until gradually we arrived at a framework for the writings. Our aim was that appreciation of the writings be enhanced by the flow of chapters and pieces. Paintings and photos were then interspersed throughout, not merely as illustrations or to enhance the layout but rather to extend, echo or embellish the themes in the writings.

The writings were minimally edited. In a number of pieces, small changes were made (usually inserting or deleting a comma or other punctuation or perhaps a preposition here and there) in order to improve readability, always ensuring that the change does not affect the content or style of the piece, or its interpretation.

—Chris Beyers

PARC

Jigsaw

We are a jigsaw of unfitting pieces
unsolvable, mixed up and mysterious
We are not the same
and not all quite interlocking
Each one is a unique shape, size and texture
We are all different colours, and we all have
various backgrounds
Some are not scenic, or funny or even sensible
We are a calico mishmash of senses
a range of experiences
We are not rigid like cardboard
and we do not fit in a framework or a border
We are a collage of collective survival
struggle
and indomitable spirit
We are eclectic, colourful, loud, angry, shy, sad,
proud, afraid
a cluster of emotions and images all in one
and yet we share this space
coming together in our differences
we non-interlocking puzzles
we collages
and we are a mishmash calico community of character
and strength

—Bobbi Nahwegahbow

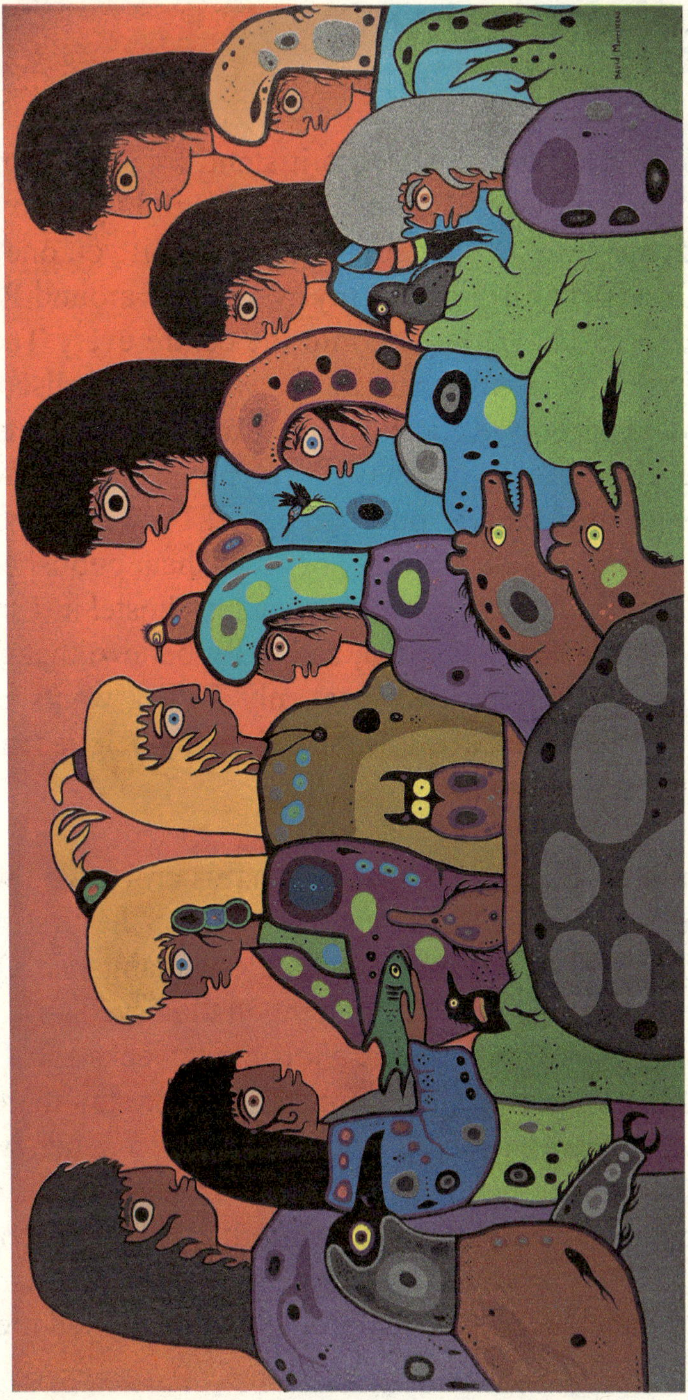

David Morriseau

PARC, Dear Old PARC

What is PARC and what does it stand for? Is it Parkdale Activity-Recreation Centre? I don't rightly know for nobody has ever explained it to me. I'll tell you one thing though and that is I center my whole life around PARC. I look forward to dropping into the centre every Tuesday and Thursday to take part in the writing and discussion groups. And now Ken and Raven are showing me how to use a computer, for I have three novels to rewrite and a booklet of poems to put together. If I am successful in these endeavors and have any or all of them published and make hoards of money, I hope to set up a hostel in Toronto, maybe in the Parkdale area, as I truly believe that this is the final project that our heavenly Father wants me to complete before He'll allow me to join my beloved mother and father in Heaven.

Now please, let me get back later to this project as I would like to relate how I discovered PARC in the first place. PARC was revealed to me by a female acquaintance, Onica, who I met while I was an inpatient on the Psychiatric ward of St. Joseph's Health Centre about eight weeks ago. Onica and I struck up a vague rapport during our stay there and although I was discharged several weeks before her, we did exchange telephone numbers and addresses. I later came in to pick her up on the Monday morning of her discharge. After taking her to the Salvation Army store and hanging around the adjacent donut shop, Onica finally led me into PARC.

I didn't return to PARC for several weeks again as I was readmitted to hospital with very strong suicidal thoughts which were brought on by matters at home and by having my motor vehicle towed away on Bloor St. All I can say is – thank God Onica was with me at the time because if she wasn't, I am sure that I would have gone berserk and would have thrown myself into the traffic. I was in such a befuddled and a helpless state as I couldn't find my beloved truck. Luckily, I had enough money on me and was able to pay the towing and pound fees and finally we were on our way.

That aside, I would like to get back to PARC, which I like to think of as my "home away from home" as I feel like it is a part of me. I know Hume, Melinda, and learned Donna's name today, and even Dave, an elderly gentleman, who had a great time strumming the guitar. I read Melinda several of my poems, spoke to Hume regarding my plans and wanting to learn how to use the computer, had a mouth-watering plateful of meat and pasta and finally left this wondrous place, known as PARC, with a gleam in my eye, as now, just possibly, just possibly, my long-planned dreams will come to fruition and I will be able to set up a 100 bed hostel for homeless people. And then finally the Lord will let me leave this wretched planet called Earth so that I can be with my parents in Heaven, who I long to be with, even now, at this very moment, while I am writing this little story.

—Kent Simard

God Bless All

Who is Jim Booth? Why he's the loudest man alive. He talks too much. He tells jokes. People say why don't you go away. Jim has friends. Nobody understands him. He wouldn't harm anybody. He tells people things about sex. Then people leave the table. If you get to know him, things would be alright. He takes life in his own way. But at times he is low. He says his life is most of the time OK. But he says to himself sometimes I wish I was dead. But don't worry, he'll be around for years. He wishes he could go back 20 years ago. Life was better. He still misses Joanne, his girlfriend, who died 4 years ago. He has a girlfriend now. But she will never replace Joanne. Everyday it gets better. And Jim lives on. Happy is when he walks into PARC. There, family is understanding. He does not want to bug some people. He just wants to make himself happy. His world is a happy one. But things are sad some days. But he will live on. God Bless All.

—*Jim Booth*

There is a Deep Hole

There is a deep hole and I don't know why

Drinking
at 14
Jail at 16
a few times
Always saying you're not gonna do it again. But ya do

Work
for 12 years
Then back to drinking again
It's always there

What's at the heart of it?
I do not know

Drink more and more
and swear you won't do it
but you do

What drives other people back? Bad relationships. Death
What drives me back: I do not know

Getting out of the hole takes discipline

Know your limits
Be nice to yourself

Being nice to yourself is harder than being nice to others
Why? I do not know

—*Jean McGrath*

My Dilemma

Parkdale has devoured my being
As I walk down darkened sidewalks
I walk through the valley of death
And darkness penetrates my heart to icy cold
The fabric of my soul rips open
To expose the raw evils that dwell within
I walk in vain conceit only to be rewarded
By allowing myself to be permissibly raped
For money.
What if a man gains the world and loses his soul
My soul has become cold my heart a calculator
So deadened have I become
That even the touch of my lover
Brings no pleasure, except for the memory
Of when my body was capable of responding
With love and longing to his caresses.
I should turn away but greed and adventure
Hold me locked fast, imprisoned.
Everything dear to me is crumbling like dust
And I know I will be left
To sit and rue in the ashes of what was the fire of my
rebellion.
I am a murderer of the worst kind
For I am murdering my soul, my womanhood
Slowly, painfully, excruciatingly, effectively.
And how can I justify it and say
That my motive is love
When all love in me is dying and withering away.
I am not a woman but a shadow of what once was.
I turn my friends into customers
And I distance my emotions from other friends
For I live in a fog of loathing and self disgust

To the point where I feel that I am only worthy
Of being embraced by the very thing
That is destroying, corrupting and tearing
My life, my soul, my being apart.
I look in the mirror, I see my hair, my makeup
The attributes that nature gave me
And I assess myself in dollars.
I look in my eyes and for a moment
I see the person who I used to be
Then I close my eyes again and turn away
The streets are calling and I go
With a glimmer of hope that someday
I will return to my true self.

—D.F. Baan

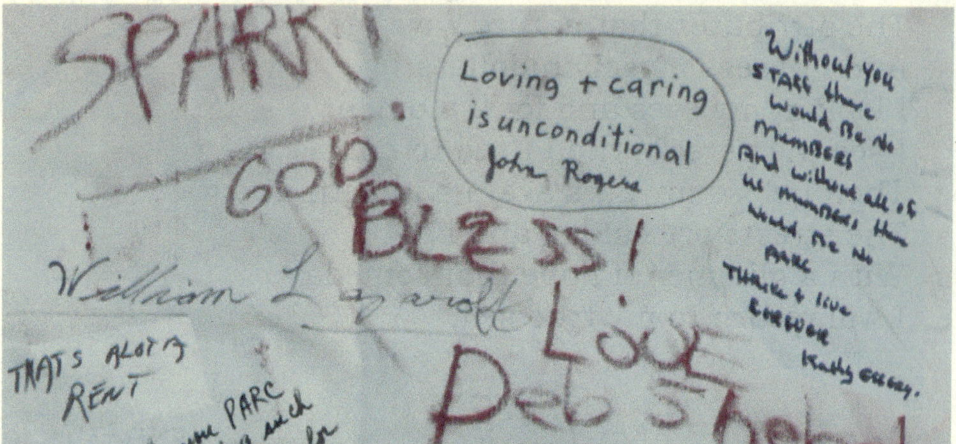

From *Volunteer Appreciation Banner*

The Members' Ship

Out there on the seas,
Tasting the wind, tasting the breeze.
Members sail on with hearts of glory.
Listen to the wind of their story.

Waves upon waves of life they face,
For everyday is a day of grace.
Onward and upward is not always the case,
But no one here is losing the race.

Be a sailor on this ship,
Be a friend when life takes a dip.
Have a coffee, eat a meal.
Take a load off and tell me what's the deal.

Together, we'll ride the waves,
And savour the days
Of enjoying the horizons, sunrises and sunsets.
Come aboard this ship and you'll find a friend in PARC.
YOU CAN BET.

—*Hillary McWatch*

PARC waiting

This place, haunted by echoes
Of other lives, in frustrated anticipation,
Where something must be made
Of nothing
            and laughter besides ...
A moment of unmediated joy,
An improbable coalescence
Of characters, jokers, prophets,
Shifting in irregular movements –
Like bats against the falling dusk –
A concatenation of voices,
By turn mute, insistent,
                        and not.

Faces bespeaking streets and streets
And in and out of rooms
Where sleep is short but slumber long;
Let's face it, more life than
Any one can stand.

The sound of shuffling along the floor
In listless inertia, through the saturnine
Semi-darkness of late fall,
                    polyester coats dangling
                    shoelaces trailing.
Now a cheerful greeting
And, amidst mutterings in the background,

A game of chess –
Over there a burst of laughter
Followed by a harangue.

Can you buy me a coffee
Or spare a smoke, friend of the high seas?
In God we trust ...
                    hey, buy me a coffee will you ...

I am
    a seer, you hear,
    I'm a seer.
But listen,
I never bow down
To the gatekeepers.

And then the dense fog of the smoking room –
Welcome sting of the eyes,
The passing of a solitary company,
We say what we say
And then hold our silence,
For words just flounder.

                              until
After some time
The meal is imminent
And it smells of meat, plus something sweet.
And now more chatter, and scraping chairs
Until gradually,
          cutlery against plates, irregular voices,

And food gets mixed with saliva
And food passes down oesophaguses
sporadically contracting,
and again, again
At tables where friends and strangers sit,
Or in couches where lonely figures hunch
To eat in silence.

Spring will come, I know.
It has never failed me before.

meantime

There is new year's eve
Where in irreverent ritual –
Keyboard calypso incantation –
Something new, between rhythm, eardrum,
and foot
Throws life into sharper relief:
Will it be renewal and promise – or
Just momentary oblivion?

But there is always a next day ...
Wrappers inside empty mugs,
Just the scraps on the carcass,
Remnants carried out in garbage bags
To be tossed into that industrial container
– ice cold, rusting,
unforgiving.

A hunched figure looks always outward:
Nothing, except a pigeon on the windowsill
across the street.
Respite from the cold, from judgement,
The city rushing out there.

—Chris Beyers

After shelter is obtained, then what?
-or-
Ten years constant

PARC has been the place I go to. The first time I went in I didn't like it and I ended up writing an angry hurt letter to the Board of Directors. Apparently the response to my letter was quite good, because it's been ten years constant.

In the early days I peeled veggies on Friday mornings for free cigarettes and coffee, while I unknowingly made friends that I still have today. As a result I have lived in Parkdale for the last ten years, the longest I have lived in any neighbourhood in my adult life. I have accessed, in different years, the food bank (former), clothing donations, laundry, computer rooms, housing help, guidance and advice from staff, outings to Camp Kandalore, Kleinberg, Centre Island, Niagara Falls. I used to "work" the coffee bar, spent time on the Board, went to the writing group, went pumpkin harvesting. During the renovations I spent days getting trained to strip and refinish wooden, glass windows. I went to many auctions at Ritchie's and Waddington's with Melinda and Kathy to buy furniture for the ten housing units on the third floor. I've eaten many, many meals at PARC, especially the Friday meal. I lost dozens of friends due to "natural causes," cancer, poverty, homelessness, lupus. I found so many little places to help out at PARC in thanks for having somewhere to go where there is always someone happy to see me. I've emceed many open stages and made thank you cards for the performers. I do special events and set decor with help from Michelle and Ruth and others. I found a place for my wild sense of humour, wore moustaches, wigs and many funny costumes, developed one of the best adult friendships through music, song and talking over good coffee; then Toby died – almost died myself.

I've been a housing advocate for seven years, untrained. Our meetings were held in the Edmond Yu room. Now I'm part of a new team of ambassadors for Edmond's Place, PARC's newest housing venture. In the last ten years I've become a visual artist, a comedian, housing advocate, better singer. I've lived in my small apartment for five years. I've learned that I am loveable, I am a good motivator, I love to help, any activity can be enjoyable, every person has a story, how to defend myself, many of our lives are tragic, and most importantly

good people are everywhere.

—Tyde

Eulogy to Jerry

I loved talking with Jerry. I have never yet met anyone who could do what Jerry did in conversation. He could, in a heartbeat express an observation or turn of phrase that was so wise and insightful that it simply took your breath away.

I used to tell him that I always felt like I should carry a little book in my back pocket so that I could write down his aphorisms; all those little word turns that left me feeling haunted, like I had just heard a universal truth. I swear to God only Friedrich Nietzche was his rival.

He seemed to instinctively recognize that words were symbols; that they were alive and could be joined with his amazing ability to see between the lines, see beyond the ordinary.

His words were always energized with the signs and symbols of the world around him. You felt this in his words and in his photographs and in his drawings.

You know from the moment I first met Jerry until the day he died I knew that he would be one of the most exceptional and unusual human beings I would ever meet.

I always thought of him as a natural prophet. He was someone who by unusual gifts and unusual experience uttered divinely inspired revelations.

He was a deeply spiritual person and this was part of his personal intensity and a source of isolation at times. There were times when I spoke with Jerry that I felt such a deep loneliness and a longing for a connection to a world that was a little more forgiving and ordinary.

But this was not his journey. So there were many hardships for him to bear as a result of his heightened sensitivity and of course the often cruel insensitivity of the world around him.

But through it all Jerry never turned away. He admired courage and he had a great deal of courage. He admired compassion and he had great compassion. He felt deeply and was filled with minor chords that could bring you to tears.

He was such a handsome man. I wish I could have met him on the football field. He was a loving warrior. I would have watched his back and I know he has always watched mine.

I met Jerry thirty years ago. It was a dark time. We walked the hospital halls together and talked and even though he was surrounded by darkness he was filled with light.

He had a great impact on me then and that has never wavered. I remember one day, twenty years ago, asking him what he would want PARC to be for him..........and he said............Well, Bob..............

I am looking for a place to recover my long lost love. Yes that is something to seek and fight for...............

—Bob Rose

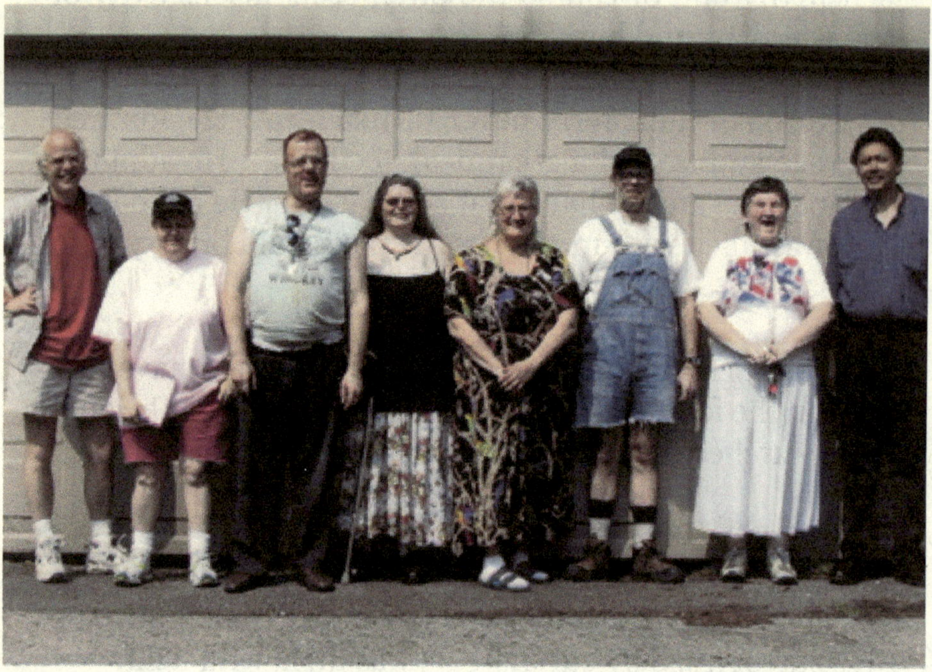

WRITING WORKSHOP

(and how we chronicle our lives)

PARC Writing Workshop

We sit in a room, today ten writers,
sometimes more, sometimes less.
We sit around two tables, jammed end to end,
motley colours of Dollar Store notebooks
box of Bic pens broken into & scattered.
Ruth wears her pumpkin-shaped Halloween hat
(she claims that it helps the flow).
Alice piles up her keys in front of her
(ritual disinvestment of all that'd weigh her down).
Rain beats against the window;
a storm is promised tonight.

What kind of room do we write in?
It's a storage room. (Society's always valued writers,
as long as they're not seen nor heard.)
We're wedged between two banks of shelves.
One side is stacked with hockey equipment:
big, bulky, overstuffed bags – do not unzip them,
the foul smell of shirts & jockstraps would knock you dead.
Large plastic containers hang over the edge
as if they resent sharing the space with us.
The other side, shelves wedged with boxes,
milk crates, rolls of paper, darkroom equipment,
computer monitors that stare down at us
like the heads of Easter Islands statues.

We write. We turn over pages in our notebooks.
We drink coffee. The Oreo cookies remain untouched.
Richard exits to smoke in the hallway
(the last time he exited, he didn't stop till he reached Winnipeg).
The one light bulb that lights the room:
it flickers & dims; it grows bright.
Traffic hums below, the streetcar slides past,

whoop of hollering as workmen hammer in the next room.
The need to write is so great we create
our own shells of silence.
Raven's shell more palpable than the green dress
she wears.

There's a heater, but it gives off as much heat
as a burning cigarette. Ken, soaked from the rain,
writes in his winter coat. We shiver,
but lightning hot hands scribble down lightning hot thoughts.
Alice, absorbed in her writing, makes a buzzing noise
like a queen bee who's found happiness
in a glorious pollen-heavy day.

We write. I'm hesitant. I'm fighting with my words.
Danielle, she's in full flow. It flows out of her in huge unstoppable wedges: life's pain, Mona Lisa's smile, poetic descriptions of willow trees, the mystique of Houdini's magic, the whole gamut, her pen glides across the page.
Wedged between the two shelves on one side is a battered blue cabinet. Only a part of it can be seen for a door leans against it.
To pass through that door to the blue of imagination!
Alice writes about the spirit of a wolf who emerges from the flames of a campfire & howls at the blue moon.
We write through various shades of light. When the words do not come, we vacantly stare at a box marked bathing suits, chessmen that randomly dot the shelves, a vase full of paint brushes, a toilet seat.
Thud/thud/thud go the workmen, then silence, it's their lunchtime.
Usually, we write for twenty minutes, today we pass thirty minutes.
Sometimes we honour that time with silence, today there are outbreaks of good-humoured bantering.
There's coughing, there's whispering, there's silence & when Donna puts down her pen & claims that she has written about happiness, we all groan & the light flickers into temporary extinction, before coming on again.

We write. Alice stares into her empty cup of coffee. She tilts it this way & that, mesmerized by the sludge at the bottom, she mutters, I should write about the sugar in my cup.

Her husband, John, rings on each finger, maroon-knitted hat pulled down to his eyebrows, face knitted in fierce concentration as he crafts each word like the jeweller who has forged the snakes of his rings.

Michelle, someone has given her a doll on her streetcar ride over, it sits on top of an old copy machine that pushes its way through the quilt that curtains off one end of the room, doll that sits behind Michelle,

doll that could be her younger self who haunted Yorkville in the sixties.

Writing. In writing we find our younger selves, our older selves, sometimes we plunk right into the middle of our present selves.

My eyes light on the red tool box that sits on the top shelf, a sticker on it reads: *The Mercedes is in the shop.* There's none of that in this workshop. We write to discover our proper size, our real selves.

It's time to read our pieces: for some, time to furiously scribble last sentences/words; for others, time to retreat to the hall for a cigarette.

Richard reads about his trip to Winnipeg, half bus ride/half hitchhiking, chilled to the bone north of Lake Superior in thin shirt & tie flapping in the wind,

Alice, the comradeship of two kittens in the last weeks of a homeless man's life,

Michelle, she's too depressed to write, how often she has written about wolves & whales, those embers of spirit which guide her in life,

Tyde, conversations of pain which break through the numbed self to at least let her know that she is alive,

Hume, I pass for the first time ever (we have an agreement that if you don't want to read your piece, that's fine, it doesn't happen very often, once or twice, but the opening is always there),

Ruth reads about being trapped three hours in an elevator when nine months pregnant,

Ken details the minutiae of his morning so far, humourous chronicles of the black & white world of his computer & his pet skunk,

Donna, a praise poem to the physical & spiritual delights of newfound love,
John, fresh from the dust of two months of renovating work, reads a many-layered piece about the renovation of the self,
& Raven, death of her kid brother, senseless, tragic death, truck that jumped over the curb, window of light forever extinguished.

Workshop: so full of life, so full of feeling, laughter, bantering, buzzing, burping, writing, reading, listening, a mountainful of trust. We enter the room, dry bumbling sticks. We leave the room, ho! we leave the room as if we were floating, the Red Sea has parted for us, we ooze from every pore the aura of having created.

—Hume Cronyn

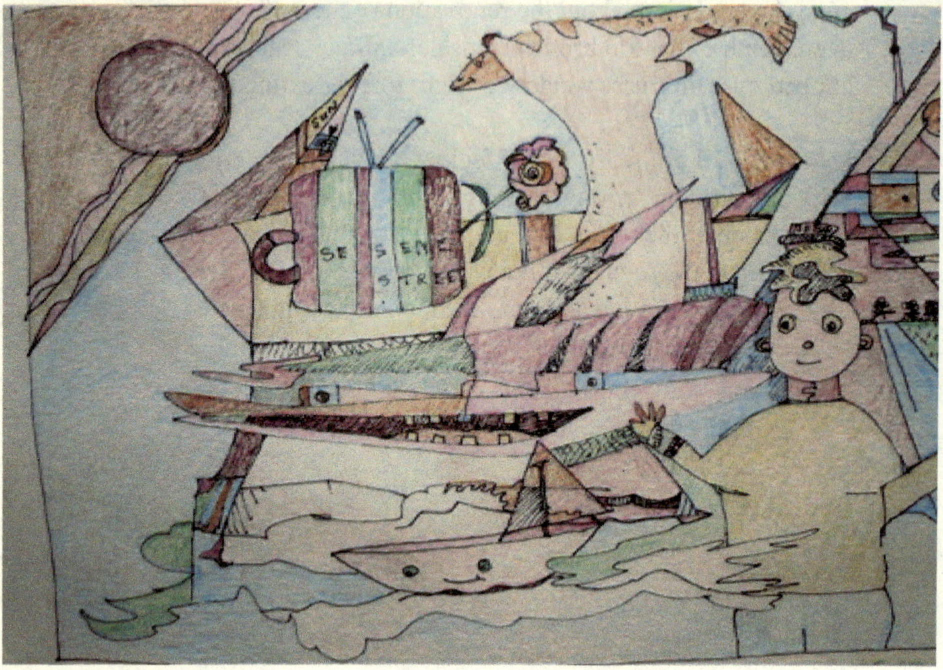

Derrick Harwin

Poets

Poets hide in the trees
You can catch them everywhere
They watch
It's their job to watch
They watch & catch whispers
the whispers of the world around them
the whispers of silence
The very air they breathe creates poetry
Poets walk down the street
but no one knows them
Poetry is what they live for, dream of & see
Poets are never free
They're born poets
Poetry is in their soul
Poets can forget their own name
take all the blame
go completely insane
but still remain poets
because that's what they are
Poets are everywhere
They hide
They cry
They live
They die
I am one

—Roberta Taylor

Thinking of Writing . . .

Thinking of writing. Thinking of other people's writing, and how they chronicle their lives. I don't write much about myself, my history, my feelings. I treat myself like nothing. I try to write fluff. I don't want to face my anger, rage, at being so unlucky as to have the life I have. Meeting other people that have had much worse lives than mine, it makes me forget that I am damaged too. Yet it makes me feel as if I don't belong with that group. There is the feeling of not belonging anywhere. I feel pain and loneliness. Am I not a good person? Why am I such a strange person? I collect books, I love to read. I also have a collection of porcelain and stuffed toy skunks, as well as a real one, who is asleep behind the stove on this overcast and rainy day. I feel sorry for myself and I despise that feeling. I haven't accepted myself yet, and I wonder if I ever will. But last week I accepted myself when I chased the seagull for fun, with no thought that I was soon to turn 40 and should act more dignified.

—Anonymous

Dancing Man

I want to write
I want to write what is in my heart
I want to express myself
in some kind of creative way
but my head is blocked
my eyes are droopy
and I'm somewhat annoyed
I can't think
there are too many distractions
too many sounds
and I'm uptight
my heart isn't open to discovering
or expressing
because I'm trying to block out
distractions.

It's not funny
and it's not helpful.

I want to write
because I can't
I need to find the words
that are trapped in my head.

The ones that won't or can't
find their way into my fingertips
and down into my pen
and onto the paper.

I need to block out the anger
but when I do that
I block out the creative thoughts
as well.

A man was dancing in front of a window
on the other side of the street
he looked at his reflection
like it was his audience.
He was singing
or maybe he was preaching
preaching to the ghosts that only
he could see
there was no mental block there
I wanted to be his audience
so I watched from my place
silently.

I want to read
I want to read about the world
outside of here
I want to travel to another place
a place that has no distractions
one that will allow me to write.
I want to write the way the man across the street was
able to dance
freely
he danced for himself
he danced because he wanted to
he danced in spite of all that went on around him
the window was enough
he only needed to see himself
within the small space that the window allowed
he was focused
and he was free.

—Renata Edan

No More Irrelevant Titles

My writing
is not
about flowers
Or the numerous
varieties of trees
that dot
wilderness and plain.
My landscape
instead
is filled
with sidewalks
& street names
The people
who populate them
and the textures
of their being
I can describe
their houses
and their buildings
in minute detail
And while doing so
take
lingering guesses
about
those
who live in them.
I look at them
myself
the people
in the collected
expressions
of our silent dialogues
I listen
to their words
Sometimes
I understand them
As often
I do not.

The reasons
why?
may vary
It could be language
or accent
or speech impediment
But
could also be
a hysterics of tongue
a voice racing
too quickly
to catch up
with its mind's
voracious appetite.
For me
poetry
is the fiercest
of all my dragons.
It emerges
unafraid
There is no enemy
that can't be
conquered
here
No fear
so strong
that it can
cripple me.
It's in these words
that I find
the madness
I embrace
The Individual
who defies
the diagnosis
to define myself.
I carry
poetry
the way
a high-wire artist
carries his pole

It takes me
through the places
in between
A bridge
to join
the once was's
and the might be's.
It keeps me present
It keeps me real
It anchors
the flights of fancy
so they don't
carry me
into land
from which
I can't return.
It allows
my mind to fly
Yet
keeps me
tethered to earth
with ink & pen.
Sometimes
this poetry
is prayer
A thing
so sacred
That it tastes
like
faith made wine.
But what it's not
is sacred scowl
bottled in fear
to be consumed
unthinkingly.
It is
instead
an expression
of human being

It delivers us
humanity
both
in darkness
& in light

It laughs with us
and at us
It reveals
our fears
our follies
and our
wondrous
ability
to survive
it all
It reminds us
how small we are
how alone we feel
And when
we hear it
from others
"In other's words"
How common
& shared
these feelings are.
It allows us
to be larger than life
Larger
than the boundaries
of this fragile room
called reality

—Raven

SUCH SORRY CLOTHES

He told me
I should learn
to clothe
my emotions
with language.

Such sorry clothes
for what I feel.

—Guy Ewing

paper, pens and pit bulls

paper, pens, and pit bulls
alliteration
candy-coloured cartons
creating contents
are we bored yet
princess pickles pretends perfection
what am i doing here?
brown betty becomes bolder
i think i am going crazy
languid lawrence's latent lividity
what are you talking about
robin rose rises rotundly
ruth's voice is reaching
sounds like it hurts
laryngitis languishes loudly
wilson writes wildly on walls
i don't want to write about lies
i don't want to write about dreams
joe jumps jamesons jackpile
i only lie to defend people
i only lie to defend myself
i only lie so i don't have to cry
alice needs a pen
a shovel in one hand
dig up the dead idea
a pick in the other
pick apart
pick apart
pick it apart

what are you writing about today
i don't know
paper crinkles
yuck
whispers in the corners
the sound of chewing
chair rumbles underneath
more chewing
a sigh smacking lips
truck backs up
streetcar clacks bell
excuse me
chair cracks
windows rattle
a cough
someone revs an engine
a page turns
hands fumble through books
pens race
you wonder what thoughts
they're playing with
streetcar stretches to a stop
too many lines on a slice of paper
hand brushes paper
another sigh
more whispering
truck idles
i can't write today
another cough
pen clacks as it is set down
a burp
excuse me

hume looks intently at the page
the box of crackers rattles
the sound of chewing
a chair moves
scraping floor
glasses sitting on a pile of books
can they see without their eyes
can i see without mine
time for a cigarette

tried to smoke my brain awake
didn't work
a fresh cup of coffee now
what was i doing?
what am i doing?
where did i begin?
oh, yes,
alliteration
plenty fancy word isn't it
sounds like i think i know what i am doing
perfecting precious peonies
is this making any sense
words taking up space
sounds like politics
i want to stretch
stretch seams senselessly
senselessly symbolizing simians
an animal that writes
an animal that thinks
think thoughts thoroughly
thankful thoroughbreds
door squeals open

resist raising rents
rack ruins ruefully
a caterpillar moves faster than this
this does not compute
this does not compute
can you fix it mr. spock
i'm a scientist damn it
not a psychiatrist
sorry wrong character
bones is sleeping
i think he's senile now
or just paranoid
no one's going to spread
these atoms
around the universe
what does that word mean?
one verse
it must have been some poem
what language was it written in?
will some linguist claim
to have recreated it
linguist lording loudly over languages
licence of licentiousness
i still have sleep in my eyes
i need to pee
we've started whispering again
i'm using my nickname again
that's a warning
time is definitely up
a yawn
i'd better take that pee
does it sound

like i'm attached to this idea
the random capture
of anything
perhaps i should use
the caulk gun over there
glue them together
glue grizzly graphic gleefully
stop me
stop me
stop me
these words are taking over
soon i won't be able to stop
i'll run out of paper
start writing on the walls
they'll find them in a thousand years
try to decipher them
and say
it must be code
coded creations carefully constituted
to conceive confusion

—Raven

A Day at a Time

Waking Up

Waking up. Oh boy, the sun's up. What time is it? Yipes, I'm late. I have to take a bath. Where's the soap? Rats, cold water. A knock at the door. Let them knock. Oh no! More knocking. I better go see who's there. I throw on a towel. Oh no! It fell in the water. I'm dripping wet. Where's my pants? Okay, I'm ready. Finally, I get to the door. Nobody there. I find a dry towel. The phone. I won't answer it. It keeps on ringing. I better answer it. Wrong phone number. I better make some toast. I burnt it. How about some cereal. No sugar. Sour milk. What a day. What a day. Time to get dressed. Darn, broke a shoelace. Keys. Where are they? Look for twenty minutes. Finally find them. They're around my neck. Next, I go to the elevator. They're not working. Take the stairs. Get outside. It's raining. Make my way to the donut shop. Closed. Oh well. Go to another donut shop. Read the paper. It's Sunday. Put my hands on my face and think, Waking up, waking up, it could only happen to me!

—Jim Booth

All of the Craziness in Between

Mouth gaping open
remember the eggs for the egg salad
my eyes burning red
oh yes, and the lettuce
Every bone in my body aching
two loaves of bread
I'm so tired, I just want to sleep
three pounds of hamburger
my mind racing with visions and memories
one bag of potatoes
I try to keep the tears at bay
one block of cheddar cheese
mouth gaping open, remember to breathe
cereal
eyes open wide
cat food
I can see all of the craziness in between
one bag of onions
my body crying out with pain
and kitty litter too
until finally I scream
Stop all of this madness and craziness in between!
I've had enough, no more
remember to get the cottage cheese

—Renata Edan

It's 6:30 a.m. …

It's 6:30 a.m. Mycroft wants to play and be cuddled and be fed. I get up and do my duty by Mycroft, then log onto the Internet and read my mail, as well as my two favorite online comic strips, *Kevin and Kell*, and *Sluggy Freelance*. Then it's off to take my medication, pop my breakfast into the microwave, then dash back to my computer to see who is on *Furrymuck*, *Area 51* and *Sluggy Mux*. Partway through a conversation my energy level runs out and I'm left feeling exhausted. I tell everyone how I feel, then take ten minutes out to rest in bed. Though I feel tired my mind is aware, so up I get, back to the computer and my friends in the virtual worlds.

I decide to try fresh air to wake me up. So I say my goodbyes and log off. Mycroft is back in bed so I leave him to snooze quietly refilling his water bowl before I head out for a coffee and to read a newspaper.

Microsoft is in trouble having been declared a monopoly. I guess someone's having a worse day than I am.

—Ken Rosser

Parental Guidance

I

Daughters eating Shreddies, full of questions. Turn the radio off quick. Don't leave it on and go upstairs. They'll be up after you, asking you to explain *human remains*.

II

Newspapers are better, but check the front-page photo before you leave it lying about. Read out the good stories over breakfast. Show the girls the picture of Marg and the pigeons. Marg carries scissors everywhere to cure their Stringfoot, snips from between their toes human hair, string, wire and monofilament fishing line, debris which hobbles them, cuts off their circulation. A bird can lose its feet or legs. She squirts electrolyte formula into the mouths of the dehydrated.

III

Pour their orange juice, hope for the best.

—Sheila Stewart

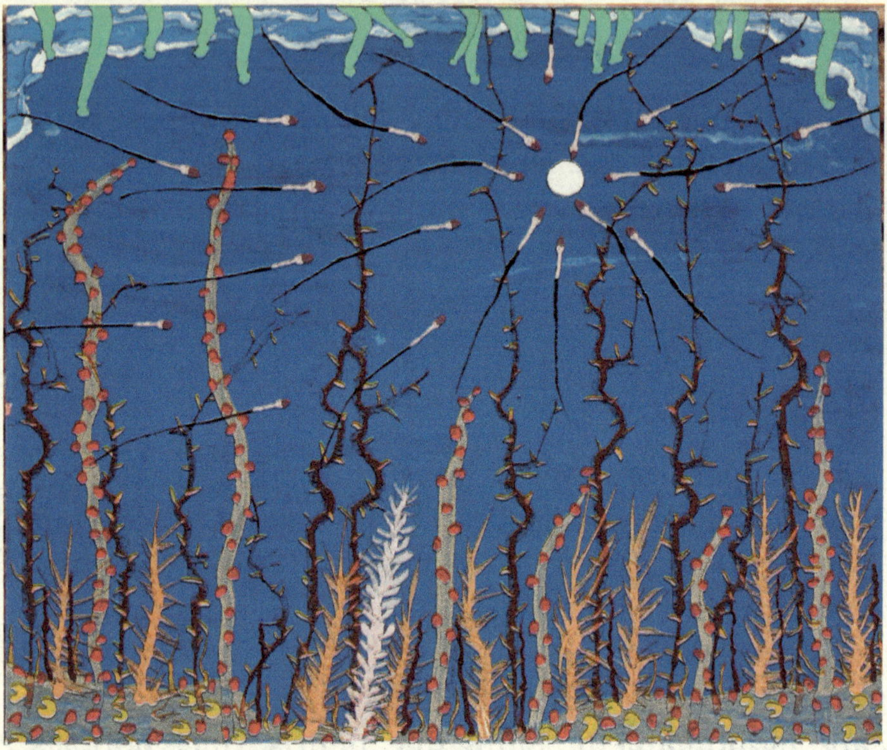

Sperm no. 17, Tyde

Facing the True

Every morning I see my face in a mirror, a face of a tired, lonely man. I ask myself, who is this man who looks at me? Maybe I have to do something to recognize the "alien." I fetch a razor, shaving cream, I put all my energy in an effort to change that face. Razor is like a sword cutting and slicing. A tiny hair left after the "hurricane" is trembling in fear. Don't worry, I promise that you can grow, be alive till next morning, of course! Morning – in which again I see the face of an old man. If I leave the beard, gray as my hair is, I shall never recognize the person who looks at me every day in the morning from the mirror – that's the true I am facing forever.

—Aleksandar Korovljevic

Christmas

These years I call it Curstmas, and wish people a scary one. Maybe I'm getting it confused with Halloween. Christmas is a time for giving, but I have little for myself, never mind to share. Those who are happy in secure jobs, they have a lot. I'm sure they don't realize how much, as I get on the phone to my landlord to tell him the furnace is off, again. Those who can buy the latest toys and tools for themselves, and family, they have a lot. I give, but it's of my skills, few though they may be, and in return I get hounded for more more more by those who have as much as I do, or less.

Do I sound bitter? Why shouldn't I be bitter, as I walk the streets in my old winter coat, scanning the ground for dropped change? It used to be that we'd receive a cost of living increase from the government at the end of the year, but they're not giving it anymore. They are not forgiving of those who need, because we cost money. Those on relief who try to give, or try to climb out of the hole of disability and welfare are faced with ignorance, maybe even superstition. When all accounts are tallied, our government and the so-called Captains of Industry say Christmas is a time for taking. Maybe it's the wind, maybe it's... Who knows? Sometimes I feel like crying.

Over the year I've again put together a lot of books for family. Fortunately, reading is a passion we all share. We talk around the dinner table of years past, sometimes Christmases past. I bring up a toy I'd wanted so badly, and actually received. I was sorry I destroyed it I tell my parents, but they don't remember that. Even in pieces, it was still one of the best toys I'd ever received. Sometimes my mother will enthuse over a book I'd given her for last Christmas, or the Christmas before, and my sister will agree, having read it after my mother and father. In this giving, there is also forgiving.

—Ken Rosser

Ode to My Cat

My cat and I have a soul connection. She follows me wherever I go and comforts me when I am down, laying down in a warm soft purring circle, contented to sleep and dream cat dreams. Her brindled body is like a zigzag quilt, unaligned stripes of orange and black here and there. She has a line on her forehead like a sacred bindhi. Knowledge, the queen goddess Isis, is her namesake. She walks regally.

Every opportunity is seized to bask in rays of golden sunshine on my windowsill or on the balcony, looking down on the poor pitiful mortals below, a bird catching her eye now and then. Thank god I have a net or she would leap. Although she cannot fly on wings, she is an angel in my heart. Wisdom and Kindness is in her eyes. Wisdom and Kindness, she gives to me an unconditional love, a gift that cannot be packaged and wrapped, but is attached to the strings of the heart. Having another living being in my life glad to see me when I come home is a heart-fulfilling, satisfying feeling, assuaging pangs of loneliness, taking away sadness.

A pet is a four-legged natural antidepressant—no side effects except hair and love.

She speaks to me in a silent telepathic language, communicating deeply with her eyes. I swear she sees into my soul. Her warm purring body nurtures me when I reach out, quelling anger and even physical pain. My life is more complete because of her.

—Bobbi Nahwegahbow

I Sometimes Am Disappointed

On January 25th I had come home after seeing my doctor. The walk home seemed so long, the air was very cold and my hands and face and feet were burning with pain. But so was my heart. I felt very scared and confused, and I didn't know where to turn to or who to talk to. I felt so all alone and desolated. I felt I could not let anyone know what was wrong with me. I felt like no one could help me. If they've never experienced what I have, how could they understand unless they've been there. Anyway, I went to the Donut Shop, tried to eat but got very sick to my stomach. When I got home I laid down about 9:30 and fell asleep. My boyfriend came home around 10:30. We talked until 2:30 or 3:00. I had one more cigarette before I went to sleep. All of a sudden I jumped so bad that I scared the shit out of my boyfriend. In my dream he was on his way to work. Someone approached him from behind and kicked him to the ground and proceeded to repeatedly kick him in the base of his skull. They kept going and going. Before I woke up I was told he was dead. Recently, all I seem to dream about is people I love and care for being killed and being taken away from me. I also see myself dying or being killed or killing myself and me being taken away from people who love me.

And sometimes when I wake up and start another day I sometimes am disappointed that I am still around.

—*Kathy Essery*

Early Childhood Thoughts

I don't want to go home today.
I walk slowly, my throat is tight and my stomach carries a lead weight.
I don't want to go home because of the way my mother shakes when she hugs me.

Mommy isn't well. There are electric currents coursing through her brain, causing explosions of white light to go off behind her eyes. She's running back in time, wandering vacant as an empty shell through our house and her present life.

She comes to me with her arms outstretched and tears in her eyes. She tells me I can be anything. I can be an angel or a dancer. There is desperation in her voice and I know she is trying to save me from being stuffed into a mold that will squeeze the life from my limbs, the same mold in which she herself is trapped and which is causing her to sink deep inside herself and disintegrate. Pieces of self slipping away and scattering at such a rate that neither she nor her daughter can keep up with the broken fragments of one life creating the next.

Do they still electrocute the minds of the young?
I thought their kind would one day be extinct but they've only grown more powerful.
Their kind, the ones who build torture chambers,
the well-fed men with smug smiles and well-tailored suits.
Their kind, who curse expressions of freedom, whose fear is thick like a cord wrapped tight around my neck.

It's too late to lay the blame at the feet of the dead.
We must treat this illness with silence. Never mind the side effects of burying secrets.

I am climbing the stairs to my front door. I am invisible, silent and sane.

—*Jessica Bonney*

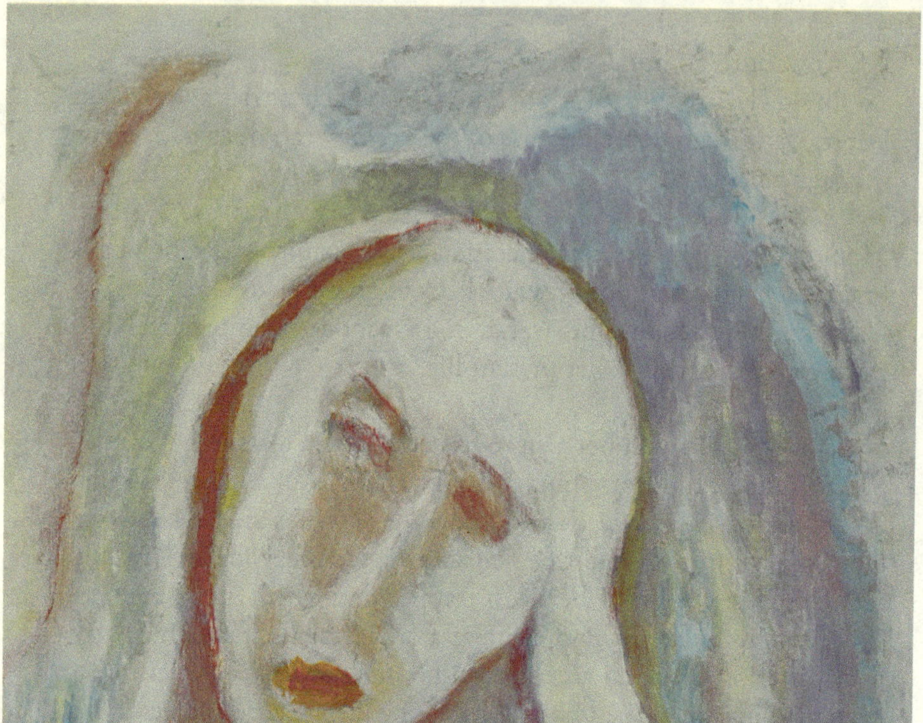

Elias Tabar

The Struggle

for

Mental Health

Mental Illness and Emotional Turmoil: My Journey

From the time I got mentally ill to now, I had to look deep into my soul and find the strength to survive. In my opinion, if a person has been suffering from mental illness for a long time, then he/she is a very strong person. I feel that suicide is a choice only if ALL avenues have been covered and nothing has helped.

....

There is such a huge stigma with mental illness. We are considered odd, strange, and unaccepted. I have felt socially isolated for about ten years. During those years, I experienced loneliness beyond belief. I would wander through shopping malls, sit down on park benches, and dwell on the past. I would dwell on my regrets and how my life would be different if I did things differently. But, you know something, it's just water under the bridge, you can't look back, you can only look forward and create a bright future. Dwelling in the past will only cause a severe depression and who knows what that could lead to.

In dealing with my illnesses, I developed interests. I would read, study, take courses, play video games, watch movies, and just keep busy.

....

The most difficult years of my life were 1999-2005. These were years at which my mental illness was at its worst. I lost my job in civil engineering and ended up in a mental hospital in the spring-summer of 1999. I was in hospital for five months. I was put on various medications, but nothing seemed to work.

Upon discharge in November of 1999, I was worse than when I went in. I spent the next few months auditing an engineering course at the University of Toronto. When I was finished with the course, I worked in construction for a couple of months, then I worked in a grocery store for the remainder of the year 2000. Again I lost my job due to my illness. In the spring of 2001, I went to Homewood Mental Health Centre in Guelph. I was tormented by some of the patients and my doctor, so that admission didn't go very well either. I have had several hospitalizations over the past six years, and all have been useless and unproductive. I found myself suffering at the hands of the other patients instead of using that time to heal.

....

Things are extremely difficult to deal with right now. People walk by me on the street and they utter: "Sicko," "Bum," "Loser," and "You're dead." I have to listen to people saying these things every day. I still have to live with mental illness, and getting through the day is like getting through a full-time job, it can be stressful. In addition, I'm still up and kicking and hoping that things will get better.

—Jason P. Perosa

The Struggle of Being Straight

The hardest part of being or getting straight is in the learning to trust yourself again. I always used to make a joke and say I can't say no twice to drugs, using the logic that if someone offered me free drugs twice then they didn't really need them and rationalizing to myself that I was taking a portion of the body pollutants away from them. I've always said you buy your drugs from the devil and pray to God that it won't kill you. That's quite true, but it's usually said with a mischievous giggle. I find it's easier to say no to drugs on the street but if someone comes to my home with drugs on them, then no is just another word in the dictionary. I've also found that one becomes a liar guised as denial–"Oh, I'll only do one piece (a twenty piece)." The lie is there is no such thing as one piece for an addict or one drink for an alcoholic.

Even with the most sincere best intentions of quitting, the first thought when money lands in my hands is to pick up one piece. That's the first lie. Like I said there is no such thing as one piece.

Then when the craving wanton jones comes, most people will seduce, lie, cheat and steal or prostitute oneself to keep the semi-oblivion that is experienced by the numbing rush.

What I meant by learning to trust myself is to not buy when I have money on me, not to give myself excuses even though I feel that I have a really good one - 12 to 17 tumours that do cause discomfort and pain. One twenty piece kills my pain for 5 hours, the rest is just head candy. The wantonness and greed disguise itself as need, therefore another lie is born. Coke is only psychologically addictive, but one becomes like a trapped wild animal when the jones comes.

When two people who are using and are in love, the love gets lost in the need and the greed, and the pipe or needle becomes the lover for both. The couple learns to despise each other and come together only for the love of the pipe.

One of the saddest things I've learned lately is that I don't have any true friends. I need to have a serious operation soon and all my "friends" know this. They are also aware that cocaine and anaesthetic means a cardiac on the operating table for me. They know that my pre-op appointment is this month and that I need 6 to 8 weeks clean. Yet every one of my "friends," even those who claim to love me the most, has volunteered to bring me drugs in quantity. My friends consider them gifts; at this point I consider every offer a shovel full of dirt on my grave. I think they lost the meaning of the word love and truly transferred their love solely and soulfully to the pipe. Therefore, in their logic, giving me drugs at this point is an act of love to them. Although I can't quite fathom it when they know in so doing I can die literally.

Therefore my greatest sadness is in the knowing that I have no true friends but I do have a hell of a lot of party friends. Maybe they all just want an excuse to buy a new black outfit. This isn't morbid; it's my reality. I have a hard time not answering a ringing phone or not answering a knock at the door. Now I have to make a resolve not to answer that door because death is knocking. I think I'm going to have to trust myself large because as it is I can trust no one else.

—D.F. Baan

ARE WE ALLOWED TO OBJECT?

I used to see a psychiatrist. I found them distant, cold, and basically unconcerned. All they pretty much did was nod uninterestedly and prescribe medications that I found were not conducive to my general well-being, and that in general caused more problems than I already had. So one day I said to my psychiatrist that it was in my general beliefs that psychiatry was to the priesthood what whoredom is to wifedom. He asked me what that meant and I told him that both a psychiatrist and a whore charge a hundred dollars an hour and that a priest and a wife do their duties free out of love and understanding. Needless to say, my psychiatrist fired me for the comment and for not wanting to take their disabling drugs that they refer to as a semi-cure. So bottom line is: it's my belief that

PSYCHIATRY IS TO THE PRIESTHOOD WHAT WHOREDOM IS TO WIFEDOM.

And why on earth is it legal?

—D.F. Baan

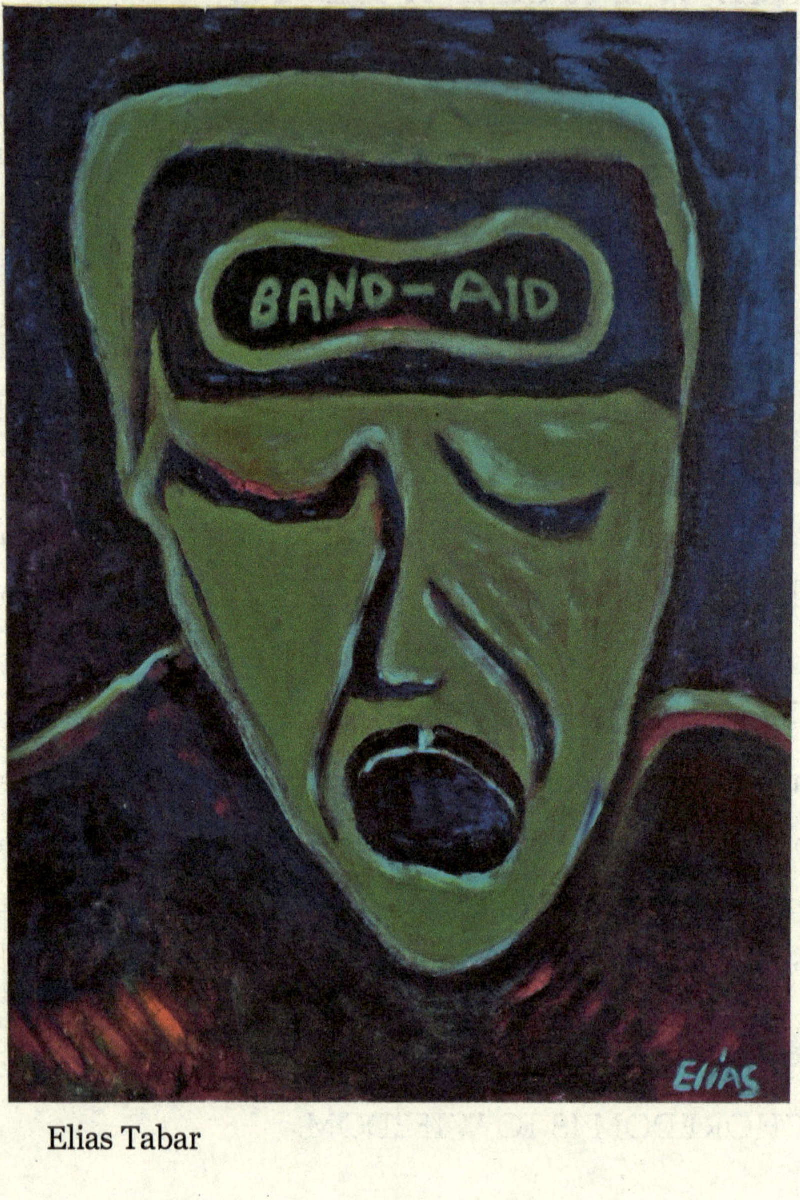

Elias Tabar

Pop a Pill

If you're tired and you got a head ache, and the sun
is shining in your eyes, and the trees look like
great electrodes,
Pop a pill.

If you're trying to stop smoking and you're craving,
and your fingers are popping, dying to hold a
cigarette, and your lungs need the pure spirit of
nicotine,
Pop a pill.

If you're lonely, and you only see yourself in the
reflection of the window, and no footsteps are to
be heard, and it seems you haven't been loved for
years,
Pop a pill,
And if that does no good,
Pop another.

If your stomach is hurting and your back is aching,
and you're about to turn thirty-four and you still
don't know what you want to do, and every time
you turn in bed you see the nothing of your life,
Well, pop a pill,
And quickly too.

If your nerves are bad and your roommate's
drinking kerosene, and you're spending the night
watching your hand jitter on the table,
mesmerized by the knuckles bare of skin,

Well, it's not the only answer,
But it helps,
Pop a pill.

If you're cold and out on the street, and all the
warm-air grates are occupied with the sad hunch
of layered bodies, and the blue scarf is tightening
around your neck,
Pop another pill,
Prozac is your house,
Valium, your warmth.

If the salt of your life is burning like sodium on
water, and every pore is an open window that
suffers every glance, and every voice is
whispering against you,
Pop a pill,
It will get better.

If you've gained sixty pounds in a couple of months,
and your tongue is sticking to the roof of your
mouth, and the loops of flesh beneath your eyes
are twitching,
Don't worry,
These are only minor side effects,
Quickly now, pop another . . .
God damn you, swallow it!

—*Hume Cronyn*

Regis' Story

They said he was out of his mind
And that they had a cure to find.
At the admissions they gathered around
And started to tell:
We give him meds, calm him down,
If he overreacts, strap him down,
Or he'll never get well.
Better strap him down.

He was a big and heavy boy,
He was walking tall.
They said, "Now look how his
Mind has taken a fall."
The doctor put the needle in,
He didn't want that kind of thing,
Code White was called again,
His acting up was in vain.

The place was known to him –
He had been here before.
After a suicide been treated
And they forgot the scar,
The infection was almost deadly
But help did arrive in time.
He got better then, and said:
"Got to see my Ma!"

They strapped him down,
He couldn't breathe, he wasn't well.
His mom said, pay attention to him,
"Because he cannot tell."
He had no history of problems that way,
The doctors came and went away.
And he got forced better mentally,
But physically not.

I met him at the coffee shop
That was hospital-attached.
He smiled at me and I at him,
He was very polite.
We talked and remembered times we've spent
In a drop-in in the west end,
And always a friendly word,
A smile would pass his face.

The hottest day of summer, too hot to walk,
They gave him a pass, to go to the park.
Medicated up to his eyes,
He thought going to mom would be nice.
Not even blocks and he broke down,
A cab and friends they brought him back.
More medication, hours passed,
Emergency and ambulance.

He laid there at the intensive care
On the brink of his death.
His body fluids made him swell,
His face distorted, he wasn't well.
His eyes could not remember when
His body blood filled and morphined.
He lost, he died there and then –
Weeks of fighting to survive.

The doctors stood around and
Filled out a form.
"God take him in your holy halls,"
Said the priest at the funeral.
The lives of family and friends have changed.
Sometimes in passing by I still see his face,
Then I remember, drinking coffee at the shop.
Regis we miss you.

— Heinz Klein

Harbinger (Unit 10)

I

Conscripted into an underwater army
of children,
each of us is chemically chained to the ocean floor.
You troll my liquid sky.
The sonar heartbeat in your hull passes over me.
Doctors in wetsuits say the word
recovery.
I surreptitiously gather sharp objects
from the ocean floor,
as our marching feet disturb grey water dreams.
Still your shadow snakes along the ceiling,
waiting.
Useless.
Your boat is too small for my revolution.

II

Comfort lives in the neon light of night.
Honest in its hopelessness.
The darkness on the edge I inhabit promises preservation,
dawn on your dock is irrefutable in its potential.
Night cycles black and you cannot/will not find me.
We only see what we expect:
Hospital gowns/uncombed hair/incoherent conversation.
Harbingers of discomfort.
Arbiters of isolation.

III

I am learning
to speak from a scorched throat.
And making the choice to die later
in this improbable place
where laughter croaks
from the nearly dead
and the profane dances on tongues.
Here failed suicide attempts have a punch line.

Hope.

—Shannon Quinn

Damn Hell

Damn hell unearthed its power, leaving me in torment and a gnawing feeling of frazzled nerves, signaling my damned state unconditionally. If I tried to seek my escape, I was re-captured into its pot of fire again and again.

I cringed at the notion to journey down the path of unknown and darkness. Where there was no light, I bowed my head in weeping sorrow. The flames arose higher and higher around me in this hot water, and my sins that I thought were few intensified my feeling of guilt. Had I listened and practiced what was right and good like a saint, I would not be here, but I am. I had tried to be my best, but Satan was at my heel. I asked so many times why, but it didn't matter.

The others in my room were spiritless and fed by demon's milk. It was putrid – it was of sick bacterias, it was carrying sickness of vile malices. It was not the milk and honey for those given promise. The feedings of the devil was tasteless and that ugly appetite only glugged down drink for an existence. I hated hell. I hated hell as it took away my appreciation. Hell, was the enemy of what man called time. It was a power that I had little control over. It, too, consumed me like an eternal flame.

Let me out of this terrible state, let me die to feel no more. But I won't find my way out – no more faith, no more hope. Hell was that void that I did not want to visit but the invitation was easy. It was so easy that it was annoying.

Heck! Hell existed not to be complementary but to beat me down unto unmerciful misery. It had succeeded all too well.

—Wendy Bassett

BEAUTIFUL HATE

AS I STAND ALONE UNDER THE RAIN I SEE THE DEVIL UP IN THE SKY. BEFORE IT WOULD HAVE DUMFOUNDED ME. I ASKED HIM WHAT THE REASON WAS.

HE SAID TO ME, "I HATE YOU, I DESPISE YOU, AND WANT NOTHING MORE TO DO WITH YOU."

I MADE HIM A LITTLE BARGAIN. I SAID, "OK, YOU HATE ME AND I'LL LOVE EVERYONE – SEE WHICH WINS."

—ERIC WOLIGROSKI

Entity

My grandmother used to tell me a story about the Entity. I would lie on my bed at night time and see a beautiful woman who'd glide through the door at me. Then, when she would go on the wall, she would turn into an ugly old woman. I was scared the first time I saw her. She was draining the fear out of me. Then I was talking to my grandmother about it. The thing she told me to do is not show fear, because the Entity lives on fear. Show her you can be friends with her, that someone can love you. The Entity would talk to me in a scary voice. Then you ask it why it tries to scare you to death. Then you say you don't fear the Entity and that it can't feed on your fear because you don't fear the Entity anymore.

My grandmother was afraid of the Entity when she was a little girl. The Entity would live off of her fear until she got older. She told me when she was a little girl she could see the Entity flying around her room. Then one day she said that she told the Entity that she did not fear the Entity anymore and that drove the evil out of the Entity.

—Alice Rogers

Anti-thesis

The memories escape my mind
But what am I
if not a nest of memory?
Somebody else's and mine

Memories of past time
and those waiting to be formed
Memories craving to be remembered,
holding on to fading minds

But what am I
if I don't care to remember?
What am I if
all I know is
I must not!

—Eugenia Cappellaro-Zavaleta

Flash of Light and Dark

When we have gone through a lifetime of healing,
we have feelings, thoughts, heartaches, and even smell.
I don't like the way I feel sometimes, and I hate myself and
the way I look
because of all the things that have happened to me all
through my life.
They say that life is what you make of it,
but I never had a chance to make it my own.
When I was a little girl, my body got bruised and cut in
many places.
I got my heart broken because my family was never there
for me.
They never loved me like they should.
They should never have abused me the way they did but
they did.
Life comes with a flash of light, whether light or dark,
and mine has been in darkness.
All my life I wanted to be a singer or recreation instructor,
but it didn't happen.
They put me on stage once. The audience booed me away.
I never felt so bad in all my life, and from that day on I
pretended I did not exist.
I had my own family that I kept inside of me so no one
could hurt me again.
But that was not the case.
Someone else came into my life and the abuse started
again over and over.
He took life and existence away from me.
From childhood to adult life, my body was never mine.

My body was stolen by people who took advantage of me
and took me from what life I did have.
They never left me alonc. Call after call.
Now I have my body back but I still have body feelings
that should not be there.
I do not know what to say. I do not know what to do.
I have been put on medication that I wish I never had to
take.
It made me gain weight and I don't like that at all.
What is really wrong with me?
Well, they diagnosed me with "Borderline Personality
Disorder".
Well, what do I care what it really is?
I know I have friends that I keep inside.
No one can take them away from me except the badman.
People go away, and it hurts inside so bad that I feel like
dying inside.
I feel they don 't love me and just want to say, "The hell with
you you're no good, you do not need to be loved, I am
going and I don't care what you say."
They say, "You aren't a kid anymore and you should be
grown up."
That is how I feel. I feel like Peter Pan.
I want to be loved and have a real mom and dad with no
children in my life.
No brothers or sisters.
I can 't hold on to my life sometimes and I feel like dying.

—*Ann Lapenna*

Tattoo

All my tattoos inside of me
They colour my organs Each one
swirls in intricacy
patterns of intimacy

Look in my mouth at pictures
waste tracts of land canvases
discarded depictions
teeth tongue tonsils gums entrance to
the dark forest
a glimpse of gullet
all carefully painstakingly detailed by
some master artist
in finest indigenous ink Each needle
pokes a hole in my skin
from within
Each a leaky faucet frustration
cannot tighten
leaking out my soul
drip
drip
drip
drip

—Raven

Being Ignored

Estranged

OUT ON THE STREET

It's a very scary scene to be in. You never know where you are going to sleep. It might be in a doorway or in a park. You just get high to keep awake so that you don't get picked up by the police. You go to the hostel for two weeks. After two weeks are over, then you are back on the street again. Then you stay with a friend for a while.

There are times when you don't know if you are going to get raped or murdered. Then you hook to get a place to sleep and something to eat. There is a time you would like to take an overdose just to get off the streets. There are times you just want to die.

—Alice Rogers

Stone Woman

Stone woman
carve me a laugh
Stone woman
break me off a piece
Stone woman
hard to touch
Stone woman
unable to speak
Stone woman
stare back at me
Stone woman
an image of who I am
Stone woman
lips carved shut
Stone woman
sits out in the weather
unfeeling, bitter
Stone woman
chipped & broken
Stone woman
forever placed in a page
Stone woman
sat on, spat on
sitting in a park

—Renata Edan

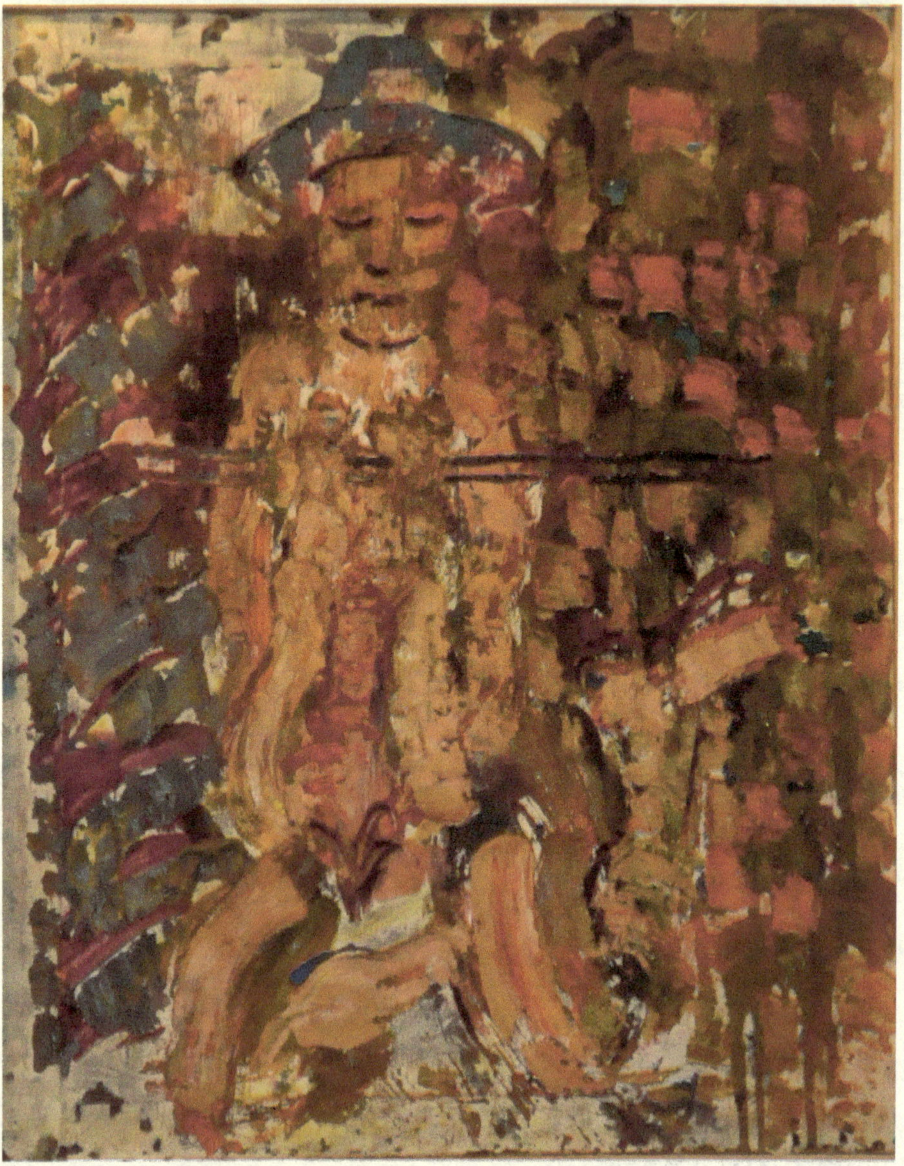

Martin Owen

The Face in the Mirror

Every day I look in the mirror when I shave. What surprises me is that the face looking back does not always seem to be the same person. Sometimes he looks tired and beaten. At other times he looks happy and young. How can the same face appear to be so many different people?

I do not understand that the man in the mirror is just a duplicate of myself, but why do I have so many different faces? Over the years I have watched myself growing and changing. Now I see a lifetime of experience in the face of the mirror. Stress and exhaustion have taken their toll and there is not much hope looking back at me.

There are times when I wonder how I have managed to live such a solitary lifestyle. Even as a child I preferred to play alone. In school I made few friends and kept to myself. When I started working I found myself being pushed into jobs where I became socially isolated. Is this what the man in the mirror wanted, or were my lack of social skills to blame?

The face in the mirror is a lonely man who seems to have accepted his fate. He never has a serious relationship, has never married and has no children. As more time passes the face in the mirror will have to deal with a very lonely old age. Perhaps the face in the mirror will one day look back at me with anger in his eyes and demand, "How could you isolate me from the rest of the world?" I do not know how to answer him.

The man in the mirror is an envious person. He wants to have friends and a family, but is it too late to change? The man in the mirror wants to change places with me for he wants to go out and meet people. He wants to go out and face new challenges. The man in the mirror would not have spent every Valentine's Day of his life alone.

As the end of the road approaches, how will I justify myself to the face in the mirror? He had such hopes and dreams. Today he is still my only faithful companion. Why did I fail him?

—Ron Forestieri

Hovering, Hovering Sea Gulls

As I sit here alone all by myself,
Just sitting under a bridge,
I am all alone in my thoughts
As is usual most of the time.

Sure, my friends, Brad and Cathy are with me,
But they are walking all around
Taking photos of each other,
While I just sit alone all by myself.

And all alone by myself,
Just sitting under the walkway,
I feel so, so lonely,
A life I am forced to accept.

But I am not all alone physically
For Brad and Cathy are here while seagulls
Are hovering over a parchment of river,
Just hovering, hovering and hovering,

Hovering down to water level
And even into the water itself,
Catching tiny minnows
And even flowing plankton too.

They just keep on hovering
And flying in all directions,
Ten or twenty feet above water level,
Then swooping down to the surface below.

And I just keep on sitting
And, as always, just so alone as life passes me by,
Wrapped up in my feelings of doom and gloom
And without any relief in my sight.

Just thinking now at 3 pm
That that man has once again
Broken into my apartment
As he chooses while I'm away.

But now I am reaching the point
Where I don't give a damn any longer,
For nobody believes me –
Neither my friends, not even the cops.

And I just keep on sitting
Under the walkway
As the seagulls keep on
Hovering, hovering and hovering.

–Kent Simard

Put a Candle in your Heart

I've been running away from
Everything I know.
Running down on empty street,
Knowing every road.

I've been crying like crazy,
Every dream I've had.
Walking up endless stairways,
And feel I'm getting mad.

Put a candle in your window,
Show me, there may beat a heart,
Show you're patient and I adore you,
Don't let me fall apart.
Put a candle in your window,
Put a candle in your heart.

I've been lost in the dark,
And I'm hiding in the light.
Searching hope and trust,
But nothing seems quite right.

I've been looking at faces,
People don't know,
And I know I'm lost,
I think it's time to go.

I've been hiding from life,
Living on the edge.
Knowing that there is not
A lot to live for. So!

—Heinz Klein

Not Fade Away

For the past couple of years, I've been bringing songs to Poetry Night. They're not poems, I swear: they're the songs I've written for PARC.

... I used to know this Lady – Lady Lady, Lady with a capital L. Makeup and poise in the face of poverty, the brutality of Toronto cops and deadbeat politicians, she was swept through with a kind of amplified glamour. She'd been living it rough twice as long as I'd been alive and still found the time to make herself up proper every morning. One morning in the pre-work stupor of too-early, too-bright, she came knocking at the coffee shop window. I gave her bus fare, we talked about the weather. The next day, she was dead. She had drank something bad, something she had found on the streets.

This song is for her, for the resilience of the body, for its limits.

maybe there is no softer landing
i mean right down at the source
what we have might be unpleasant just truly unpleasant

maybe there is no better contract
the figures all shake out the same
if there's a foot or two of ice here that's all the difference

& i know a lady who swallowed a bottle
a brown horse
a fly &
a bag

i know a lady who swallowed a birch tree
                                        wet concrete
                                        sore motives

& died of what we leave lying around
try pretty hard // do what you can //
try pretty hard // some of us just aren't gonna make it

everything looks as if it's sleeping
if you look from far away
and if we fall may we rise dripping: defeated & angry but glit-
tering

this may be our one great triumph
this may be our only triumph
if we fall may we rise very hard: defeated & ashen but glitter-
ing

'cuz i know a guy who could swallow the seasons
                                        the joints between never and
when

i know a guy who could swallow his own arm
and still manage a grin
as if by miracle

try pretty hard // do what you can //
try pretty hard // some of us just aren't gonna make it

—Griffin Epstein

Cut Back

They cut the grass today
Cut down, cut back
Cut in its prime
Cut for standing tall and proud
Cut for simply being

Being no more

Dead — but never smelling sweeter or stronger.

—Charlene Forsythe

SOCIAL
JUSTICE

With Apologies to Allen Ginsberg

There is no one to howl anymore
there are only fierce whispers
inside hollow fibreglass or metal shells
with the pulsing of gas-filled engines.

There is no one who can shake his fist to the sky
and demand an answer
There is just subtle sameness and more dangerous weapons
but with no voice.

There is no one to pray anymore.
There's just a box that implies truth about the way things are
but hides reality like it is shameful.

There is no one to howl anymore
there are only bleak predictions
and intolerable suggestions from those in power
who don't really care.

There is no one to howl anymore
except maybe me, but I'm too afraid
I might not stop.
Besides
there is no one to hear me howl
who would even understand
at what it is I am protesting.

There is only the pounding engines
subtle anger
frightened whispers
hollow prayers from a box
bleak predictions from power.

So why do I try
why do I try to howl?
Because maybe
I am the only one who can.

—Roberta Taylor

If I had a million dollars . . .

If I had a million dollars I could put it in the bank and live off the interest. I could travel to conventions and meet in real life all the people I've met over the Internet.

Maybe I could afford a house and furnish it with books, computers and skunks . . . and perhaps a new bed too. Maybe money would make me brave enough to raise my voice about government policy failings. But is one million dollars enough to raise the volume of my cry and so shift the social policy makers?

If I was rich, would I become infamous?

If money makes you powerful, would they cut off my power? Perhaps it is better to just live life quietly . . . but I'd like just a little less misery, please?

—Anonymous

Mike Knox

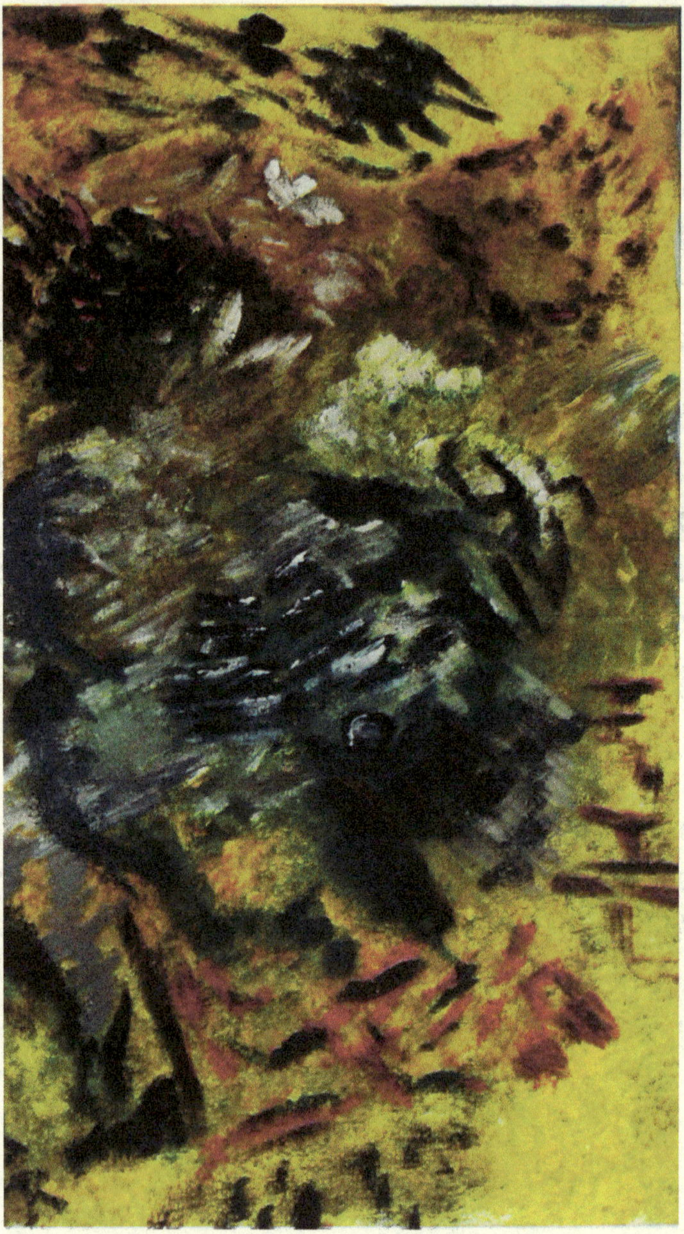

June 15, 2000

An explosion of Rage & Violence
An Anger that pierces the soul
And I'm afraid
Afraid of the horses
That are trying to chase us down
Afraid of the pepper spray
        & tear gas
That threaten to leave us incapacitated
Afraid of the volley of stones
        bottles, and cans
That fill the sky
        like toxic confetti
Afraid for the bleeding, fallen
        victims
    and those who are taking
        care of them
Afraid of the mounted animals
        who charge and attack
        the clearly marked triage
                        stations
Defying the basic convention
        of the civility
        they are pretending to protect
Afraid that this is only just a premonition
        a foreshadowing
        of an even darker future

Afraid for the carefully cultivated
pacifism
That is both my identity and my goal

Afraid that I'll lose myself
and become the very thing
that strikes terror in my soul

I watch as people tear up
the paving stones
I watch as they hurl them
down again
To break them into hand-
sized pieces
I imagine their weight in my hand
and the fleeting satisfaction
I'd have
if I were to strike
the enemy down
A satisfaction
that would dissipate
the moment I saw
that I'd done harm

The only question left then:
was it fear
or conviction
that held my hand?

—Raven

Once Upon a Time . . .

Once upon a time there was a young man in search of accommodation which he eventually found under the roof of a wicked landlord. Now what the landlord didn't know was that every night the young man turned into a skunk and ran about the apartment eating the mice that infested the building.

One night the landlord came into the young man's apartment and saw a skunk . . . He left quietly, but the next day he confronted the young man, saying, "I told you you couldn't have any pets here!" The young man responded that he didn't have any pets, that the skunk he had seen last night was actually he, the tenant, magically transformed. "How can this be?" asked the landlord. The young man opened the medicine cabinet, disclosing an assortment of pills. "This is how," said the young man choosing a pill from a vial, which upon taking it the young man turned into a skunk.

"Why a skunk?" asked the landlord.

"Because that's the largest animal that can survive here, considering how much of my income your rent takes," replied the skunk.

Now the landlord began to scheme. "What other animals can you become?" he asked.

"Oh, a lion, a tiger, or a bear, if I wanted to," said the skunk.

"Ah hah," thought the landlord, "I can turn myself into a tiger, scare away my tenants, then put the rents up into the stratosphere!" Then, he took down the vial with all the warning labels on it.

"No! Not that one," cried the skunk, but he was too late.

The landlord, on taking the pill, turned immediately into a mouse, and the skunk had a mid-morning snack.

— Anonymous

Homeless

Does Jim Flaherty understand the meaning of the word? No. Unless you have lived homeless, you have no understanding of the word. He should walk a mile in their shoes before making that kind of judgement. Just because someone is homeless doesn't mean they are less a human being. Human beings are supposed to be protected by the Canadian charter. Are they now going to take away some of those basic human rights?

Throwing someone in jail is not the answer. It would be the same as what I watched on a program called *Amnesty International*, where women in India were jailed because they married someone their family disapproved of.

Instead of adding to the already existing problem of prison overcrowding, build low-income housing. Why turn the Wellesley Hospital site into condos for the rich? The rich can afford to build their own house; the homeless cannot.

Yes, it may be a shame that there are homeless people living on the streets of this great city, but don't make it a literal crime. Yes, mental illness may be one reason for a person to become homeless, but if the proper support services were in place for these people, maybe it could have been avoided. Some low-income housing units allow rent to be paid directly to the landlord, insuring the rent is paid.

Institutionalizing homeless people is not the answer. If their doctors don't think they need to be, what gives you the right to say they do? But for some, how about group homes that also help with independent living and teaching them skills they may have forgotten. It would give them their dignity of having their own space with someone to make sure they remember their medication when needed.

The homeless are people. Not just grimy faces wearing raggedy clothes pushing shopping carts. They have feelings, a heart and a soul. They deserve the dignity that everyone else seems to possess.

—*Brenda Swainson*

Eviction

Tears of pain
run from my eyes
throwing away my memories

Tears of pain
run from my eyes
packing what little I can save

Tears of shame
run down my face
not asking for a place

Tears of anger
run down my face
as family turn their back

Tears of fear
run down my cheeks
as I pull my cart onto the bus

Tears of fear
run down my cheeks
as I enter a hostel for the first time

Tears of fear
run down my cheeks
as I ask for a place to rest my head

Tears of sorrow
pool in my eyes
as I say goodbye to new friends

Tears of thanks
spring from the pool
as I say goodbye to the staff

Tears of joy
run down my face
as I enter my new home

— Brenda Swainson

House that Loomed Thirty Years

I went to see Entirely Martha.
The stars were grazing on the pasture of night,
the street lamps circled with blue orbs.
I knocked on her door. There was no answer.
Strange, I thought, she could be out in her garden,
but this is not the season for gardens.
So, I knocked again, & not hearing a sound,
I slipped through the door.
The cat was drinking a cup of tea.
The floor was covered with milk bottles, ice cream cartons, puddles of
Tia Maria, pages torn from encyclopedias,
& other assorted objects of the night.
Red string was everywhere:
in twirls & gads & unseemly knots
it threaded its way from room to room.
I followed it through the kitchen & up the stairs & down the hall &
past the bathroom.
My legs felt weak, I shouted,
"Hey, Entirely, what's all the string about?"

The door to her bedroom was closed.
I turned the knob.
She was lying in bed, pressed against the wall,
wrapped from head to foot in red string.
"Oh no," I said.
"Yeah," she whimpered, "bad case."
"No," I said, "last night I threw the dice of salt across the blue flame,
it's time to turn back the cloud of doomsday thinking.
Come Marth."

And we cut out across the grey streets,
across the blue of late-night lamps.
We saw spoons lying on the doorsteps of the hungry,
we saw lawns brown with the cries of abused children,
we saw verandas with the empty chairs of the lonely,
we saw broken dolls planted in the gardens of battered mothers,

we saw red skulls hanging in the windows of the mentally ill,
we saw faceless dice marking the doors of numbered soldiers,
we saw giant clocks in the crumbling garages of factory workers,
we saw camping magazines scattered on the sidewalks of thc crippled.

And turning the corner at the moon's singing,
we walked down a street with blue ashes,
our footsteps glowing white as day.
The trees spoke like birds in the wind,
the sun rose in four directions.
We came to a house of red brick:
thirty years it loomed in the blue sky.
It had a hundred doors
swinging on hinges of lockless air.
There was a door for thc blind man with his street-hard hands,
there was a door for the single mother with her three colicky children,
there was a door for the drunk with sickness frozen in his beard,
there was a door for the girl with her dove-like feelings stabbed by a
    hundred looks,
there was a door for the man whose mind was stretched in the forked
    tree,
there was a door for the crack addict who carved his initials in death's
    body.

And there were a hundred windows that opened like flowers
& the lonely cloud with its broken mast sailed in,
the bird that couldn't sing flew in,
the red leaf that had lost its branch floated in,
the tears of a hundred widows streamed in,
the song of tortured prisoners drifted in.

And inside, Mary, who has lived in thirteen boarding houses in the
    past ten years, always wanting to have her own kitchen but never
    having it, not even permitted to make a cup of coffee, she now
    cooks culinary delights from all over the world, & every night
    housemates gather to eat their fill, laughter ringing out because for
    once they know that tomorrow they will also eat.

And Alice, who wants to write stories like Edgar Allan Poe, but says that she can't because he's been dead for over a hundred years, she starts a printing press with paper made from dirty rooms, cockroaches & unscrupulous landlords, & her stories are passed from hand to hand.

And Peter, who once was a top salesman & has spent the past ten years walking half-steps in fear of the dagger-man epilepsy, he now designs stained-glass windows, which people from all over the city buy, changing the day of white hurry to splendours of colour.

And Lewis, who has spent five ghostly years haunting his grey-lined room playing endless games of chess against himself, sometimes so torn by his twelve voices that it would take him days to move a pawn, he now takes on the weight of flesh & blood as he plays championship games with friends equal to his skill.

And Boyd, who cannot put the night to bed, afraid that the dark-clawed tiger will seize him by the neck, afraid that the great white bear will squeeze him to death in polar arms, he now looks after the house's pets & they wander freely from floor to floor.

And Dorothy, child of God, so her father called her until he left her when she was five, for years she wore a coat of shells, & her husband left her after five months, & all the shells were broken because she had fallen to the pavement so many times blind drunk, now the children run up & take her hand because she is a pearl of gentleness.

And Shawn, who left early from work, excited that his family was picking him up, birthday surprise, he was ten feet from their car when a truck came barrelling down the street, struck it, killing his wife & two children, years he rode the horse of death in flea-pit hotels, now he has kicked his habit, maybe he talks too much about the love of Jesus, but he tends the garden like a family.

And John, mind of a five-year-old, endlessly he wandered streets to
escape basement-room loneliness, for years he had not talked
because no one had talked to him, now he stops people on the
stairs to acquaint them with neighbourhood news while he
blows out smoke rings as eloquently as any Proustian sentence.

And Richard, who frantically travelled highways to track down his
adoptive parents, a trip to Vancouver could skew to Anchorage,
he never located his parents, but now, late in life, he finds himself
in tireless commitment to Fauve-like paintings & the singing of
Hank Williams songs, destination which he shares with all.

And David, who saved his wife from an ocean suicide, only to lose her
to a back-alley overdose, son who was born crippled & became a
lawyer, waste that is life & is salvaged, he now rescues from the
street all manner of furniture & refuse which he recycles &
embellishes to delight us with imagination's turn.

And Entirely Martha called this home,
& I called this home,
& some days red string still wraps around us,
but mostly the blue flag of sky joins us to others,
& once or twice the black anchor of despair
has pulled the house to the bottom of muddy water,
but all hands have bailed
as the light struggled to reassert itself.

—*Hume Cronyn*

DO WORKING GIRLS REALLY NEED A PIMP?

The dictionary says that a pimp is someone who solicits clients for a prostitute. This definition is outdated and not accurate in today's street life. Most pimps are usually the working girls' boyfriend who makes sure she goes to work, eats and sleeps when she needs it so she won't look dragged out on the street. He makes sure other pimps stay away from her and settles the score if any other street people mess with her. However, any smart working girl knows how to avoid these situations in the first place. Few pimps stand beside the working girl if she gets busted, they hide behind the excuse that they don't want to be implicated in a living off the avails charge.

A pimp takes most if not all of the money and so-called manages it for her. Usually most of the money goes on drugs and a smaller portion on rent – if they do have a place to live at all. Due to the lifestyle they eat mostly takeout food lacking proper nutrition.

The working girl is bombarded with negative reaction to her occupation. The Church, the law and mainstream society in general do not accept her in that lifestyle. Few working girls have straight married friends for the wives don't trust her around their husbands and believe that her lifestyle is a bad example for the children. Straight men don't want to be with a working girl for a variety of reasons. They want a real one-on-one relationship based on monogamy, loyalty, love and tenderness and can't bear the thought of someone else touching their woman. Another factor with a straight man is that he'll take a lot of flack from his straight friends about her and of course he'd be terrified of diseases.

So the working girls' companions are the other people in the life, other prostitutes, drug dealers and users, alcoholics, and pimps, as well as their dates. It's a pretty closed-in world that can collapse in on her. That's when a pimp moves in. He knows that she's suffering stress from all sides and offers her an emotional oasis. He tells her he accepts her as she is, tells her he doesn't judge her, he makes love to her for more than the ten minutes in a car like she's used to, and in general exploits her vulnerability. His reward is that he gets the money, the drugs, and he gets complete control over someone who pays him to do it. He makes sure that her self-esteem stays at a low so she won't walk away and some use physical violence, threats, fear and or guilt to keep his meal ticket. Emotional blackmail and manipulation are his primary tools, as well as his sex.

But think about it girls! A working girl works the trade all day long to get HER money and then hands it over to some man so he will love her and make love to her. When a working girl has a pimp there is only one whore in the house and that's the pimp. As soon as she hands him the money, she becomes a trick. He's paid well and he is smart. She has to see several clients a day to get the money together and he only has one client – the working girl – and he gets paid large!

No man's dick is that good girls! Think about it – for real! Check yourself and if you want or need to talk to someone, we are here at: PARC, 1499B Queen Street West, and . . .? You are not alone. We will listen and we will be there for you. I do know what I'm talking about. I myself was a working girl for years and I also left an abusive relationship in September of 1997. I'm still trying to put my life back together. It's a work in progress. You can too! You are welcome.

We aren't going to tell you to quit the trade – only you can decide that – but we are saying you don't have to live in fear and tolerate being exploited. We can assist you with housing, medical concerns, legal matters and friendly confidential counselling in a nonjudgmental atmosphere. Think about it!

So bottom line is: Do working girls really need a pimp? Hell no!

—D.F. Baan

The Modern Day Slavery

My forefathers had fought against slavery.

I believe it's time to wake up and smell the coffee, shake out the cobwebs and fight back; because history is repeating itself.

Today the shackles and whips are drugs, alcohol, cutbacks, etc.

The masters and overseers are the pimps, drug dealers, temp agencies, armed forces, police, Children's Aid, government, etc. They are raping us with greed, dishonour, promises, etc.

They are stealing our pride, self-respect, independence, etc.

They are killing us with ignorance, lust, hate, etc.

I'm tired seeing the strong picking on the weak!

I'm tired seeing the government stealing from the poor to give to the rich!

I'm tired having the parasites like the pimps, drug dealers, dishonest police, politicians, etc., roaming around!

I'm tired hearing about Children's Aid stealing children from the poor to be sold to the rich!

I'm tired seeing the children suffering and being sent out on the streets to get money to support their parents' dirty habits!

I wish that things would change for the good in this world!

— John Rogers

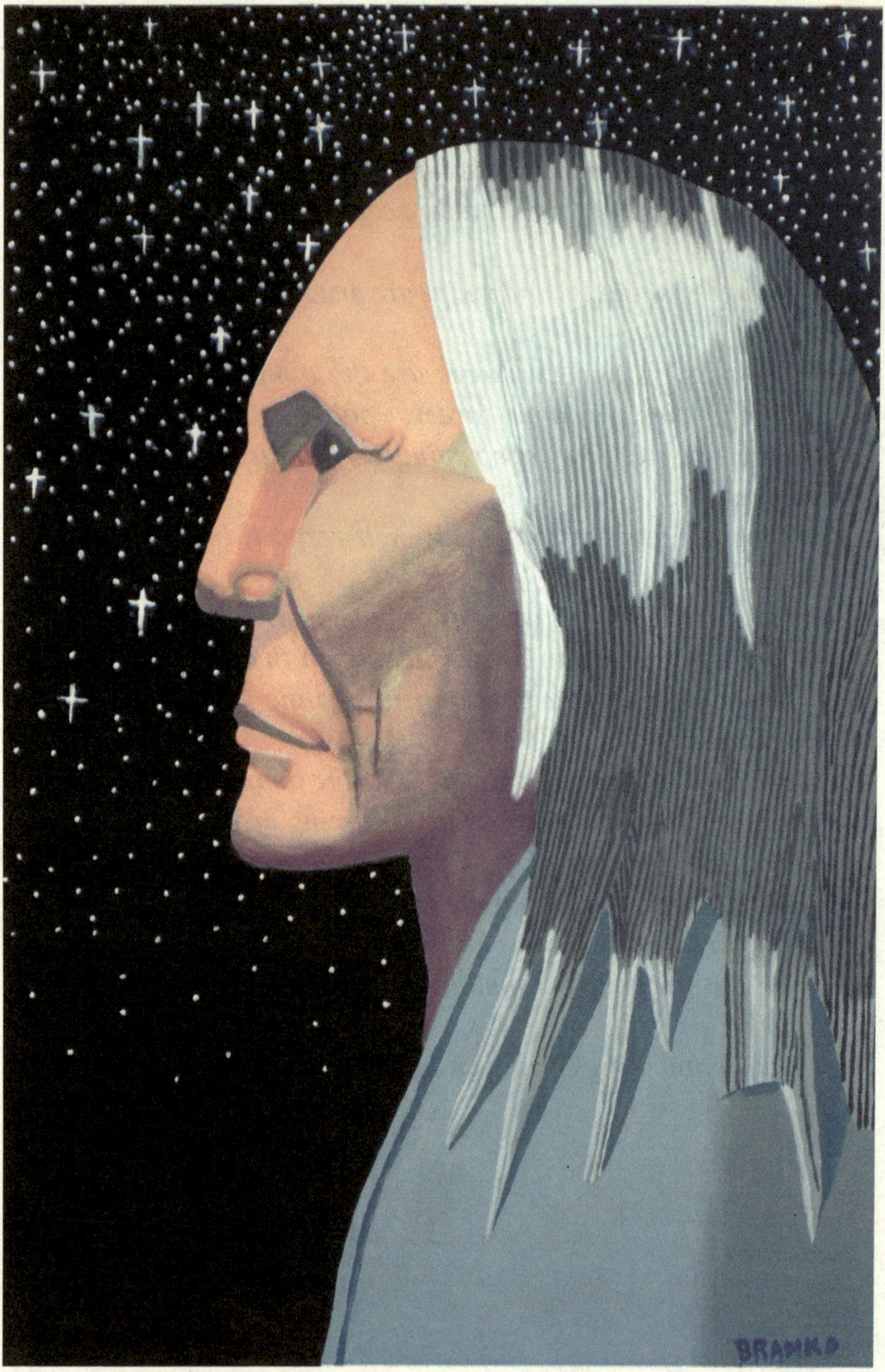

Branko Aleksic

Native Prayer

They took our Native tongue language away.
They teach our young the English language.
They took our culture away,
Teach the young that their culture is wrong.
They take away our forest
so we don't have the herbs to heal our sick,
so we have to have modern medicines to heal our sick.
They took our kids away from us
because we were teaching them about their culture.
Police would hurt us because we were different,
lock us up, throw away the key.
They would make laws that we couldn't do our special dancing.
They took our way of life and destroyed it
by taking our kids away from us
and teaching them
their way of life.
We must bring our culture back to our young ones.
Young ones can understand their cultures and carry on their cultures.

—*Alice Rogers*

The Horn

For Randal Dooley and all the other children who have died at the hands of violence

Horn – The word of the day. Something to write about.
How can I write about Horns when so many things are going on around me, around us?
And yet how appropriate that the word would be "Horn" (something that makes a noise to warn us to move or get out of the way.)
A noise to tell others that we are in a hurry.
A noise to let everyone know that someone just got married.
A noise that wakes us up.

I want to sound the horn.
I want to make a loud noise to wake people up, to sound a warning.

Beep, Beep –
Honk, Honk,
Da, Da, Da, Da, ta-Da! awiiga!

Listen
Can't you hear what's going on?
Have all you plugged your ears,
have you all gone deaf?
Why can't you hear
the screaming children,
the broken hearts,
the voices calling out for help?

Why can't you hear
the bones cracking
the tearing of the skin
the soul so broken
the tears falling
the eyes
screaming in pain?

Why can't you hear
the slamming of the doors
the banging of the walls
the head hitting the ground
the slapping
the punching
the moans and groans?

Wake up!
Everybody
wake up!

The children are dying
and no one can hear their sounds.
No one is listening
to the pain and torture
that is around them.

I want to sound the horn.
I want to give a warning.
I want you to wake up.
Do something.
Wake up and listen.
Sound your own horn.
Make it loud.
Gather together
and make a sound that no one can ignore.

—Renata Edan

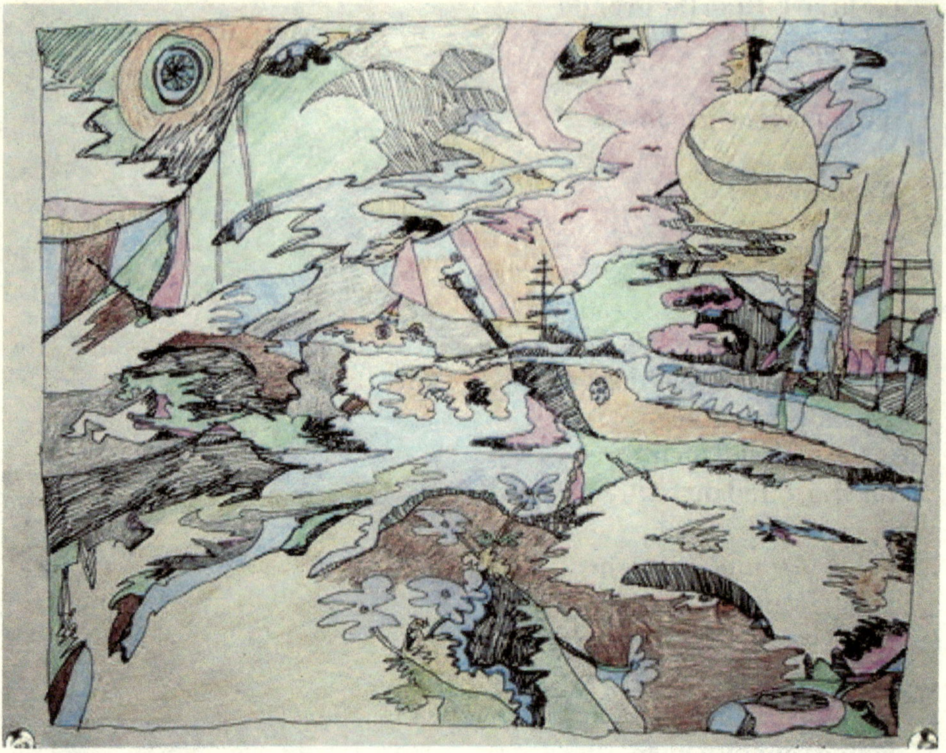

Derrick Harwin

THE LIGHTER SIDE

Things I Thought About While Going to the Washroom in a Public Toilet.

If the gravity on earth gives out could we adapt to living lives crawling on our bellies? Or would snakes hunt us?

Did we design ninja stars to look like starfish?

I wonder what a plane would sound like if the engines sounded like church bells?

Wouldn't it be funny if after all my ranting about corporations I got a job in one?

I think that boys and girls go through puberty earlier because of the chemicals we put in chickens to make them grow faster!

If you wake up fast enough do you think that you could see yourself still sleeping?

Imagine if I walked down the street and randomly stung two people with scorpions. Do you think that they would fight each other?

It is my firm belief that chickens act as forensic experts by constantly asking us to look at the ground. Why we don't is beyond me.

How does my hairstyle define me socially?

If the moon is made of cheese, then which company owns its distribution rights?

What is the human race?
Why are we racing?
Who's winning?
Who's the sponsor?

If an idiot can be President of the United States, then why can't I be the Queen of England? Would I have nice legs if I wore a dress?

Man, I wish I was a dung beetle, what a life!!!!

If humans were dogs, would we have to sniff each other's behinds before engaging in conversations with each other?

Anyway, I've thought long enough and I'm laughing at the urinal wall, which seems so un-amused, so it's time to finish.

Thank you for sharing a little bit of my private life.

—Tom Poray

Empty Heads

People frequently complain about others with empty heads. But an empty head can be a useful thing. In an empty head you can store phone numbers, the sum total of your bank accounts, or obscure computer commands. There's also room for your likes and dislikes so you can get along with them.

The problem is people with full heads. There's no room in a full head for a new idea, a new view, or a different world view. People don't look for new experiences or new information because their heads are already full in spite of there being almost nothing in there. Why in the presence of someone whose mind is full is there such a feeling of vacancy as though no one was really behind there, behind their eyes?

—Ken Rosser

Body Parts

Head is like full moon.
Hair is like flaming star.
Ears are like fans that keep you cool.
Nose is like a ski slope that people ski down.
Mouth is like a rubber band that stretches for miles.

Fingers are like green Jell-O that bounces.
Arms are like branches on a tree.
Legs are like a mushroom that grows.
Toes are like pieces of rotten beef that smell bad.
Bum is like a pumpkin with a smile.
Teeth are like bad sticks.

–Alice Rogers

Mapping My Body

A starting from head to toe, my feet are like clawed tendrils with symbolic hippogriffs tattooed on them. My calves are like wooden trunks. My knees are my greatest investment, like hubcaps – a liability to my legs. My hips are like marionettes in a puppet show, twisting and curling from manipulations. My abdomen is an apology, holding my intestines, rolled and full of disgusting bacteria, like an army of crazy peasants at the market, bartering for goods or perhaps domination for a reason to exist. My chest is like a bagpipe, blowing and lifting in and out, celebrating the breath, the sound of life, coursing through all the heavy grooved veins connecting to my heart; my heart of hearts, the centre of my body's earth, a volcano of joy and passion, a volcano of hot love and fruitful emotions of bloody success; my heart, a volcano of pulsing unsaid feelings. My shoulders are lighthouses, beckoning structure and solidity. My neck is a crane for my skull and brain. My brain is full of grooved impressions, conduit, the orchestra of existence in my body, holding the highest office of body/mind politics. My eyes represent the window of my soul and are also symbolic gestures of the working of my whole body. And lastly, my nose is a scout, a sniffer, electing joyful or silly encounters and experiences with savory or offensive smells.

—Amy Ness

My Christmas Poem

It can't bc Christmas today because I woke up and there was no snow on the ground.

It can't be Christmas today because when I had a shower all my Christmas spirit got washed out of my head.

It can't be Christmas today because I spent all my Christmas money on a pair of socks and have no gifts for others.

It can't be Christmas today because I opened the window and a gust of wind blew all the ornaments off my tree.

It can't be Christmas today because the turkey decided it didn't want to be dinner and ran away.

It can't be Christmas today because Santa told me personally that I'd been a naughty girl this year.

It can't be Christmas today because the carollers sang my joy of giving out of my ears.

It can't be Christmas today because I do not want to eat the last chocolate in my advent calendar.

It can't be Christmas today because the angel on the top of the tree is making fun of me.

It can't be Christmas today because when I walked outside I stepped in reindeer poop and got it all over my shoes.

It can't be Christmas because Santa called in sick.

It can be Christmas because no matter what things happen there is still love and Christmas will be happy.

–Chloe Cronyn

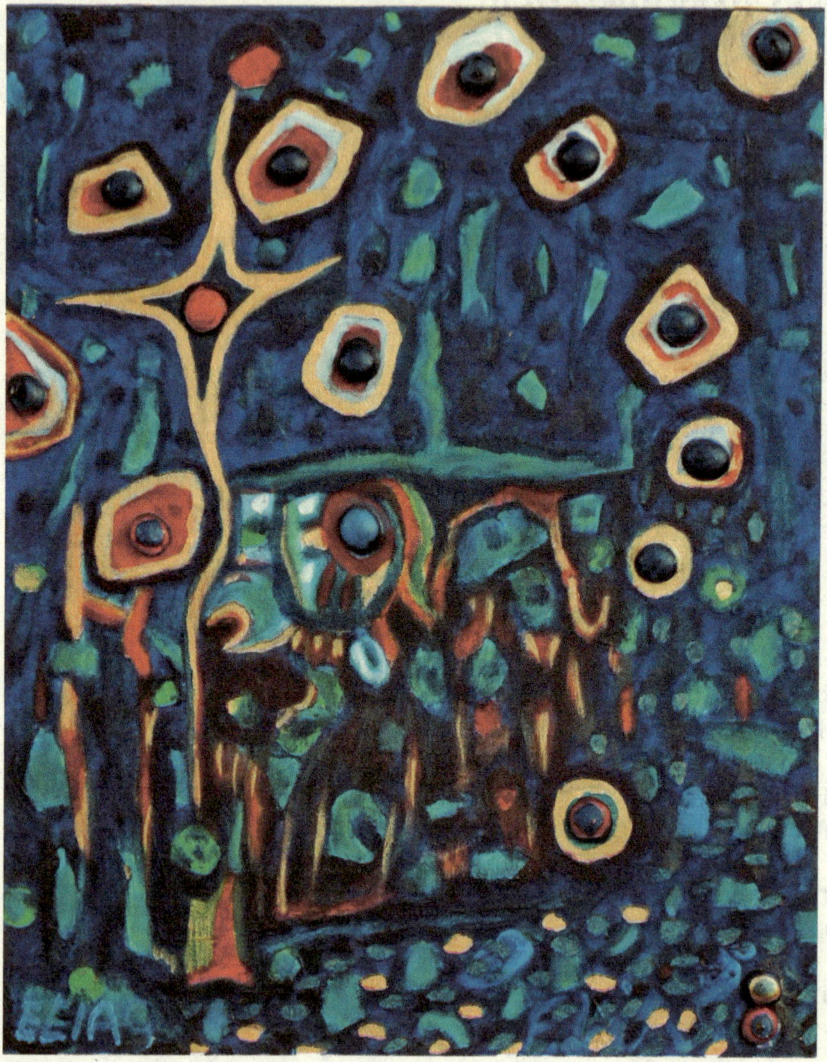

Elias Tabar

CHUNKS OF JOY COOKIES

One day at writing class I saw some cookies and I thought, what if I became a cookie?

So first thing I was just some chemicals. Then I was added with some other things. Next I was hot and soggy. Then I was put in a machine putting me into a mix of pastry. Then I was cooled. Next thing I was with other cookies. One by one I was put into a bag, next into big bags. Suddenly it was dark. I was rocked back and forth. I heard noises. I was cool. I wanted to get out. Then I was moved to somewhere else. I heard people use the cash registers. Then I was moving again. I sat there. I was still wanting to get out. I heard voices again. I was finally out! A big hand picked me up. **Hell no, she's going to eat me.**

Well, bye-bye world.

—Jim Booth

Hockey Cat

Deftly the roll of tape goes skittering across the
hardwood floor

Like a puck on the ice
1234 little skates send him in
a fury behind the net to deke out
the goalie and I hear a miaow
pronouncing the score

BAM !!!

The puck ricochets off the TV
The legendary black and silver uniform goes
WHOOSH!!!
into the deep end
tirelessly he retrieves it yet again

The play goes quiet for a few minutes?
APPARENTLY the referee has called a penalty and
our
fearless feline
has to sit it out in the box (the litter box that is)
Again the puck goes flying into the hall deflecting off
the
heater BAM!!!
He head checks himself on the front door
but secures the loot
between sharp teeth

Back to the living room centre ice the puck drops
one on one play action resumes
(I'm in net of course)

He shoots
The puck flies into the net and under the couch
GAME OVER
Our hero struts around searching for a sunny nap
after the tummy rub down in the locker room (by me
of course)

—Ken Cromie

Satan's Salad Bar

On Friday, July 3rd of 2005, Julie, Scott and myself (who work for Green Thumb, a PARC business) went to one of our clients' home address (to remain anonymous to protect the guilty). As we were doing the garden in the backyard, there were weeds everywhere and it looked like a salad bar gone wild. There were dandelions, chickweeds, ragweed – name it, they have it, except for the ones you smoke – and we called it the garden of Hell. Whenever I'm mowing the lawn, some of the blades of grass kept popping up at me like they were happy to see me. I think it's because of the adjustment of the blades of the lawnmower, or someone fed the lawn viagara.

On Friday, the tenth of June of 2005, Charles and myself went to the same house and it's an honour to be trusted alone – other than Charles – with sharp objects other than my wits. The lawn looked more like straw than grass because of being dry! Those poor little blades of grass looked like they've had their tongues hanging out, were panting because of the heat and carrying little picket signs saying the owners are unfair – Please water us. After I'd finished the watering, it looked like they were bowing down to me saying thank you. I think it's my imagination, or too much sun.

—John Rogers

THE COCKROACH

Why do cockroaches have so many offspring at a time? What message does nature give out to make that little pod open? Why do they like my house so much when there isn't any food or garbage to play in?

Why does my landlord look at me and think that I don't mind living with them? How come when they dry out and die, they get crunchy and have the same colour as my hair? What are they looking for in my underwear drawer? Are they crawling in there to die or does it happen unexpectedly, leaving them in a death dance without tribal traditions to send them on?

Do they scream when they're on their backs with their legs wiggling or are they deliriously stoned on roach killer seeing visions of a really dirty place that's humid, Spa?

Why can't I think of some good use for them when they are so plentiful, like . . . start a club. I could call it the "Dead Roach Club." There'd be a hotline. There'd be a whole advertising campaign I'd run. "Too many roaches, call the 'Dead Roach Club,' we'll (but it would really only be me) come over, kill and collect your roaches for free," then . . .

I could have another line. "Tired of telling your ex to shove it, worried 'cause your boss won't give you a promotion, call 1-800-blah...blah... and we'll send them a beautiful wrapped surprised box filled with ... you got it ... Dead Roaches. Only $39.95. All major credit cards accepted."

—Tyde

Da Fridge

Is that light always on? What happens once you close that door and the magnets lock? Is the army of mould battling for the hamburger from last week? Do the hotdogs like being in a tiny package? I believe when you close the door the parsley and celery go on a date. Sometimes I can hear the sauerkraut and relish arguing over who tastes better on food like hamburgers and hotdogs. But that's just my house. How about yours?

—Anton Kooij

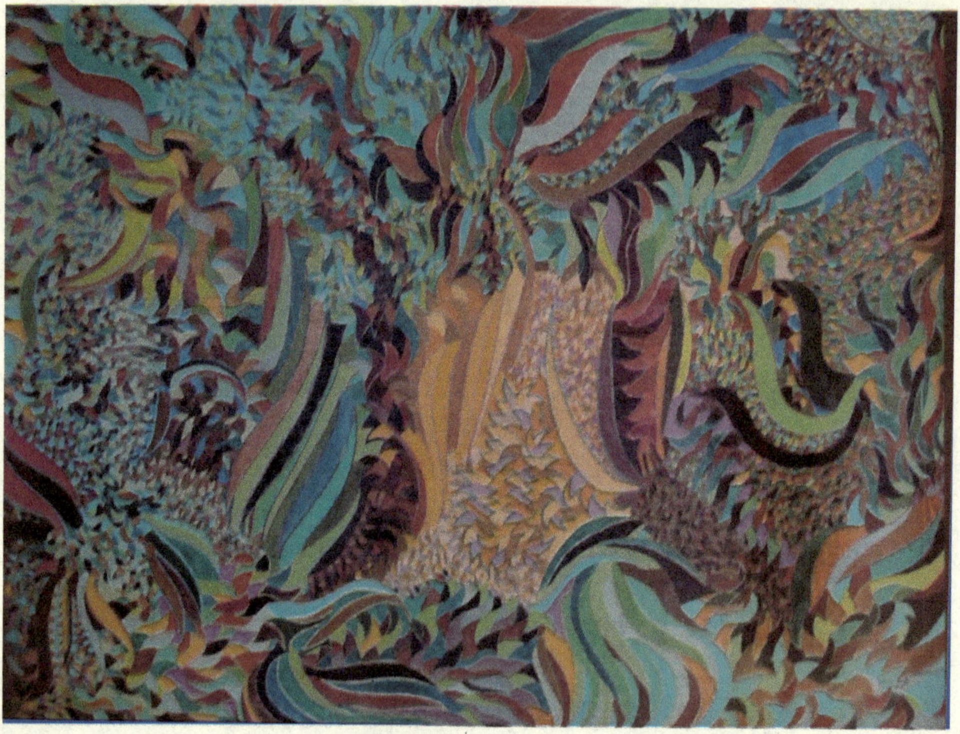

Garden of Eden, James Smith

Secret Places:

Safe Places

In Your Face

Sometimes the world has a closet.

When we were kids we played hide-and-seek in the big old house in the city. Counting to one hundred, Mom stayed in the kitchen while we scattered for a place to hide. Upstairs in the guestroom, the closet seemed the best place. What was there came from places we as children hadn't discovered yet. We squeezed our way in and scraped the door shut and stood in the gap between the musty old winter coats and the stolid pine smell of the doors. And before being found there was another world opened to us. The time that had been regimented and controlled for us to be in gradually slipped away, and slowly we heard the world deprived of colour replaced by our imaginings. The smallest sounds crept through our wooden barrier and gradually we listened to the sounds outside our new world as if for the first time. And under the door the light streamed in bands of moving light cascading from objects we had never seen before. Here we were a hidden camera locked in time. Waiting to be found.

—Ken Cromie

Secret Places: Safe Places

As a child, I spent a lot of time in my room. When I was ill with colds or asthma my room was a warm steamy place where I was left alone with a black and white TV (I'd festoon the room with wires to augment the aerial and pull in odd channels). Then there were books. Books are a great place to hide. Everything and everyone disappears as the world of the book takes over.

My books were kept in the closet because of my allergy to dust. Sometimes I kept myself in the closet. Hidden in a corner of the topmost shelf, I could be alone with my imagination for hours. I'd climb on a chair, from there to the bottom shelf, kick the chair away to throw off the scent, then, using the shelves like a ladder, I'd ascend to the third and topmost shelf and sit in the most shadowed corner opposite the water tank.

Today, my safe place is my apartment, though the landlord has the key and won't hesitate to peek in and try to discover what I'm up to. I'm only up to here in books, computers, stereos, stuffed toy skunks (and one wolf), electronic parts, and my secret pet, who has safe places all over my apartment, including in the kitchen, where he comes for attention and food.

—Ken Rosser

Safe Places

In PARC I feel safe. It's a place to relax, read a paper, drink coffee. Someone comes to me with a computer problem. I go through my price lists, explain how their problem might be solved, write out instructions. I leave because I need a quiet place.

I go to the donut shop. I read. I buy a coffee, and a sandwich. Then I'm told to leave. My 20 minutes are up. I wander over to Goodwill and enjoy looking through other people's castoffs. I step aside when someone wants past. Wait while a group wanders slowly past, map-less and without direction. I can almost hear them moo. Finally I'm backed into a corner by a woman who uses her baby's carriage like a weapon. I flee.

Back at home, I'm safe. It's as quiet as I want it to be. There's a knock at the door, the landlord wants to see if my space is tidy. No, he's not there to fix the plaster, or the pipes, or help me with the cockroach infestation.

Under my bed it is dark, it is quiet and clean. There's a gentle crackling sound. But I'm not coming out because, finally, I can't be found.

The floor is growing warm.

—Ken Rosser

Inside

Disease here is a thin voiced storyteller.
We inch forward in line,
children hanging on every word.

In this medicinal procession
the violence in me is unseen
by the frequent flyers of these hallways.
I lag behind a cluster of one-night Christs,
who always jockey for the lead.

The rest of the procession has moved forward.
Received their paper cups filled
with the hues of Easter basket tablets;
pink, blue, yellow.

In my starved silence,
it arrives
strong and dry,
a sparrow that thrashes
wildly with panic,
beating up against my sternum,
inside of me.

Nurse comes to see
why I have stopped in the middle of the hall.
Wings batter my ribcage.
A shy smile that belonged to me years ago comes back.
"Feel here" I say to her,
"and here."
I place her small hands on my side.
"It's the good inside of me."

–Shannon Quinn

Someone

Where do you go when someone
leaves you?
The best place is to hide
No one bothers you but you
You're in your own world
You can wait for them to come back
But they won't
You can dream about how to bring
them back
But they won't come back
So you find someone else to take
their place
But what happens when they leave
You start dreaming all over again
And then back into your hiding place

—Ann Lapenna

Wolves of the North

Wolves of the North, why do you run away? I hope to keep you safe from harm and I know that I am like you. I follow the dream always. I look forward to where I'm going. I listen to your call for help.

I talk to you as we play hide and seek. You run quickly and your eyes are fiery red, sometimes a yellow-green. Your freedom is very important to you and I. We have a freedom and a friendship between you and I. I have lived your way many times before.

The wolves call ow, ow, ow. Many packs of wolves hang around me. My heart is the wolf of my childhood. My babies have been the Guardians of my life. We are one. You must stay with me, my Guardian, till you are free. I see you growing with many different paths to travel to the North to where you become my Spirit Wolf.

The Spirit Wolf came to see me in my log cabin. My log cabin is where no one can get to, unless you're taken to it. It's very silent where all come to the Circle of Life. There are many wolves who come around the log cabin. The Spirit Wolf comes into the log cabin and just stays for awhile, then leaves. My home is feeling very much at ease.

So he walked away from the log cabin. The Spirit Wolf is very beautiful. No one can come to where I am staying because it's very deep and very far. Only the wolves know the way in. My Spirit Wolf is not far away, he's always near me.

This is my heart, my childhood and my life. There are many wolves in the forest. Beautiful birds and the Spirit Wolf return to me.

Beautiful Spirit of the North, Guardian of the North. You are free to come once more to my heart, my childhood's heart. My love and your freedom is my wonderful Spirit White Wolf and my Guardian.

May you live long my strength, my childhood friend.

—Michelle Caron

Homeless Kittens

My name is Fred. I live in an old cardboard box under the bridge by the bench. It all started when I was fishing on the beach for my dinner and I saw this black, white and orange kitten going around my feet. Then I began to pet her on the head. I told her that she shouldn't follow me because I had no home to go to. But she gave me a funny look. It was just like she was saying that she was homeless, too. So I picked her up and put her in my bag. That was to keep her warm and safe until we were under the bridge to sleep. When we got to the bridge, I let her out of the bag. Then I gave her fish. I put her under the blanket on my chest. She was so happy to be there, and I could hear her purring happily. I decided to call her Patches. I went to the corner of the street to panhandle for food, while Patches was sleeping in the bag. Then I went to the store to get Patches some cat food and I went back to the bridge. I opened the cat food with a knife and gave Patches some cat food. Patches was so happy with the food.

Then we heard a sharper scream near the bridge. There was man whipping a little black and white kitten. The man left the kitten on the bench. Fred couldn't see any movement from the little white and black cat's legs. It looked like a dead pair of socks on the bench. Fred decided to call him Socks. Fred told Patches that we were going to have a guest for the night. Fred put the kitten in with

Patches. Patches treated it just like it was one of her own. Then he was walking down to the bridge to go to sleep. They were both sleeping under the blanket on Fred's chest.

In the morning, we saw a policeman coming down the bridge. My kittens jumped into the bag and were very quiet. The policeman asked me what I had in the bag. I told him, "I have two homeless kittens." And he told me, "Watch you don't let them die in that bag." The policeman went on his way down the bridge. Then Fred decided to keep Socks. Fred told them both that they kept him alive. The kittens were Fred's friends. Fred found a baby blanket on the beach that he put down for the kittens in the cardboard box to keep them warm at night time, but the weather was getting colder and Fred died of the cold and snow.

By the way, there was a lady who was walking along the beach. She heard the kittens crying in the cardboard box, wrapped in a baby blanket under the table. There was a letter left on the table that said we are homeless kittens. It also said our names are Patches and Socks. The lady was so touched by the note that she took the kittens home with her and kept their names. She gave the kittens a lot of love.

—Alice Rogers

Untitled

Think about the happiest day of your life
Remember the happiest day of you life
Would you remember the saddest moment of
the happiest day of your life
Of course not
There were no sad moments
It was the happiest day of your life
If we could recall how it was the happiest
day of our life
Every day might be
Today could be the happiest day of my life
& right now it is

—Roberta Taylor

Christmas Tails

No! No! It can't be Christmas!
What have I done to deserve this!
Will Santa be good to me?

My family has grown in the last three weeks.
First a girl, then a boy.
Now, as of Tuesday evening this week they are five.
Five grown cats live with me!
Three in the bedroom and two in the living room.

Soon it will be Christmas.
Five Christmas stockings hanging on the walls.
All full of treats, catnip and toys.
Five little cats - well maybe not that little -
Lying under the Christmas tree,
Waiting for Christmas Eve,
Saying, "Daddy daddy,
Please, please, can we sit on your knees?"
The snow falling outside like a torrent of white
And fire burning close to my feet,
"Daddy, daddy, can we have some of our treats."

I finally finish my eggnog.
The taste of the nutmeg still lingering on my lips,
Two of my boys wrapping themselves around my hips.
I lean over and pick up a bag of half-eaten treats.

The two boys jump off my knees,
"Daddy, daddy, yes please, yes! yes!"
My other two boys and their sister comes running to me
"Yes daddy, daddy, please please."

I hand out the treats
Taking care not to step on their feet.
"Oh daddy, daddy, we love you.
We are happy that we live with you.
Daddy, daddy, some catnip please."
So up I get, pull down a small pack
from the top of the Christmas tree.
I spread out the catnip on the carpeted floor.
They roll in it and over it
Being merry and jolly with one and all.

My boys know that Christmas is near,
And a happy, happy, grand new year.
The Christmas Tree is all lit up.
The lights all colourful and shining in the night
In the dim light of my humble abode.
So this story will always be told
As in days, ye in days of old.
All cats over the globe celebrated Christmas
the way this was told!

—Terence Eustace Williams

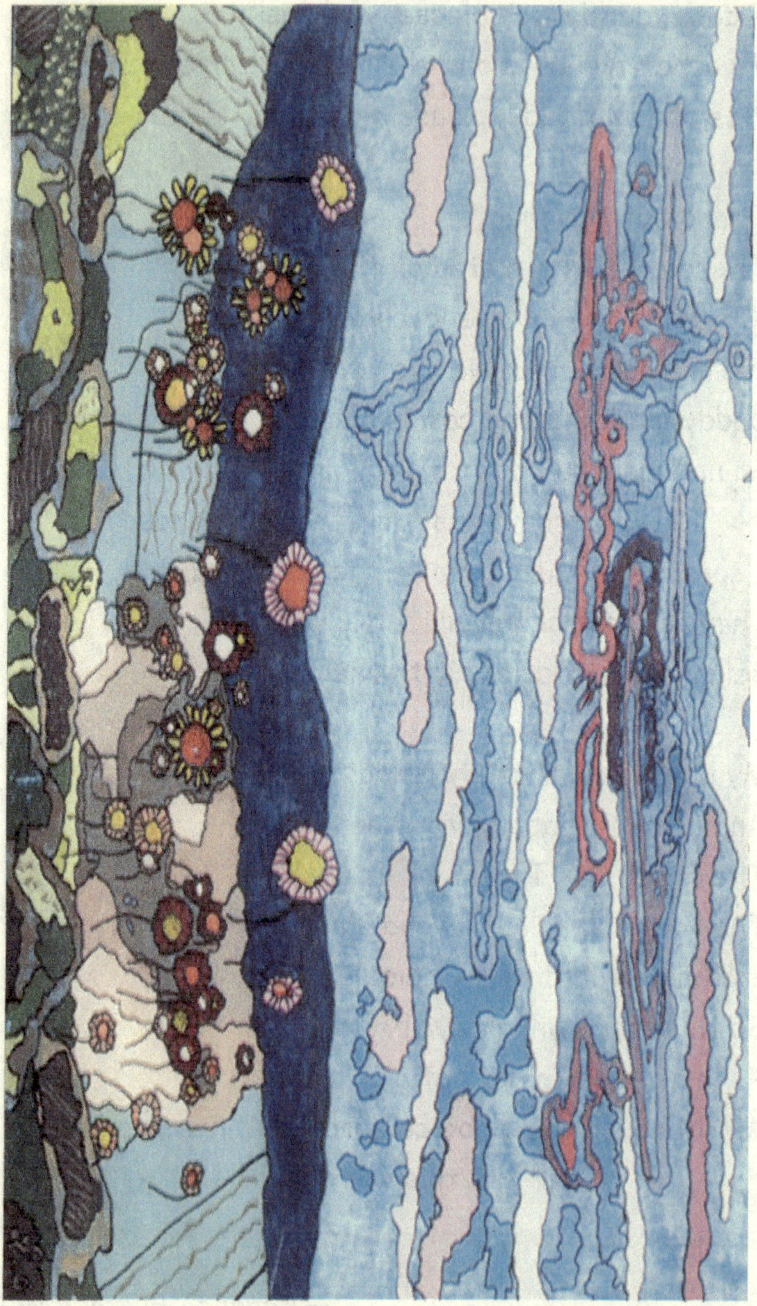

Yellow Submarine, Tyde

Nature's

Solace

Mohawk creation story

Geese
caught her, falling,
on their wings,

held her,

brought her
gently
to the ground,

as we must hold
a tiny frog,

a fish,

a deer,

or any creature.

They flew to her,

not pausing to consider
the woman's entangling hair,

her strange
featherless skin,

not doubting the
power of wings.

—Guy Ewing

Sunrise

The ocean. The water. It's a new day. The beach is alive. Silence is in the air. The birds are soaring like there is no tomorrow. Mother Nature is passing her wand over the water like kissing each one. In the middle of the ocean the waves are big, with the waves getting smaller when they get to shore. The sun is shining on the water. Birds are high in the sky. What will the day bring? Swimmers, people walking, kids playing on the beach, but before too long it has to end. Bye sun, so long wind. Kids go to sleep. Everything is quiet. The birds are heading towards the sun. The sun is falling into the ocean. Mother Nature has tucked everything in for the night. The moon is here to guard nature. But don't worry, Mother Nature will pop up like a toaster tomorrow. Now lay down. Everything will be O.K. Bye-bye, have a happy night. Don't let the bedbugs bite. Good night.

—Jim Booth

THE WAVE

THE WAVE IS COMING ON STRONG
I WONDER IF IT WILL MAKE IT
I WILL HAVE TO TRY AND MAKE IT
IT IS COMING CLOSER AND CLOSER
I HAVE THIS FEELING INSIDE
MY HEART IS BEATING FASTER AND FASTER
IT IS COMING
IT HIT ME LIKE A FLASH OF LIGHTNING
THIS WAVE MADE ME BETTER

—ANN LAPENNA

The River

This river is my blood that runs through my veins, and my whole body feels this river go on and on for miles and miles. She brings me comfort and strength as I stand on this huge rock. She runs through this beautiful green pine forest as I stand above these rapids looking down from this high cliff wondering how high it is.

It is about one hundred feet, or fifty feet, or eighty feet? Who knows or who can tell me? Maybe no one knows.

But picture me jumping from this cliff and becoming an eagle and flying above these green pine trees. Picture me diving and grabbing a large salmon swimming up these rapids and eating this salmon on top of the cliff. It's wonderful to be a White Arctic Wolf or even a deer running free and becoming each one of these creatures of the Earth.

It's just one of those things in life. These are free creatures, and all these things in life and these creatures are god's creatures. And they are all beautiful.

–Michelle Caron

Summertime

I am floating, I am singing.
I am cool and it feels so blue.
The blue is for us. The sun
is the best.

Sailing. Sailing. I am sailing.
The trees are for us. The fruit on
the tree I love. The sun burns
me but that's okay.

The house is full of food.
We always love food.
Food. Water. Water is what
we need.

The grass is green, green. The
sky is blue and I'm not blue.
The mountains are beautiful
to climb and to enjoy.

—Ramona Mack

Please Give Me a Moment

The waters gently touch the rock. I want quietness. Let the God inside me rest for a while. It's too much, too deep, please give me a break and let me come back to myself, like the waves come to the rock. My soul is sore by talking about you. Please give me a moment of quietness and let me go back to me, as these waves go back to the mother lake. I want peace. Maybe I want quietness and maybe emptiness because if we are empty we don't suffer.

—Luis Filipe

Pines

Like brushes

I imagine them
painting the sky

My arms

are branches
to the sky's

tides of
light
heat
cloud

in the
afternoon
I am still

at dusk
I bow
and shiver
in the wind

Looking down

from an airplane
I see the forest
holding to the earth
tenderly
like moss

like us

Solace of trees

fire in the brick
                solace of trees

ache of longing
                solace of trees

anger in a small room
                solace of trees

—Guy Ewing

PARC Camping Trip (II)

I am a silent man.
Once I loved to talk
beneath the cracked lights
and the pale flow of beer.
I would talk and talk
till the morning streamed through the windows.
Now I listen,
and sometimes when I listen
I feel like a speck of sawdust
that is raised up and exalted like a westward-leaning jack pine.

This is the story of words,
words sung,
and sung,
they flew up like fireflies
and lit up the cold sky.

We sat around the campfire –
Margo, Michelle, Bob, Rick, Eric and ten others.
The fire flickered; faces glowed;
shadows were held back,
like dogs on leashes about to leap.
And we were embraced,
embraced by the warm fire,
embraced more fully than any lover could ever hold us.
In the city we are called glueheads, schizophrenics, nutbars,
    manic depressives, loonies,
but out here,
out on the point lapped by water,
out beneath the stars and the pine trees redolent with resin,
we sit on rough-hewn logs,

sit shoulder to shoulder
and sing.

We sing for ourselvcs,
we sing for the person next to us,
we sing for lives that have been a parched throat.
Our voices, at first, reticent mumbles, awkward attempts,
voices oppressed by medication, hunger, homelessness,
voices that have not sung for years,
suddenly they gain strength,
and gaining strength, we populate the sky with the words of our lives,
we populate the sky,
for once the sky is for us,
not for the skyscrapers, traders of flesh, merchants of venom, parasite lawyers, cop-out politicians,
but for us, the sky is for us!
Each word is our signature,
and it is carried by the wind:
some child will wake up in Iran and hear our voices,
some mother living in a Yangtze River cave will catch a fragment of our song,
some old man, once battered by Chilean truncheons, will fall asleep to our song.

The song finishes. Each one of us feels a quiver of fear. What will rush into the gap?
Nothing! Those fuckers who sit in hospitals and label us, those unmerciful children who dog our heels, those callous ones who ghettoize us,
they are held at bay, for once we are what we are,
not labels, but the undeniable gift of soul-life.

Bob thumbs through a battered old folk book, looking for
another song.
I sit next to him. He mumbles, points to a song. I say yes.
He strikes a chord, the first words.
Michelle and Margo, next to me, pick up the words,
sing the most delicate harmonies, like wounded hummingbirds.
I follow up. Eric joins in, Rick, D.J., Brenda,
our voices gain the confidence of Gothic cathedrals,
'Corrina, Corrina, where'd you stay last night?'

The ancient forming of the rocks calls us a gathering of angels,
the wind through the trees calls us a window of light,
the lapping of the water calls us the venerable pilgrims of
experience,
and the sky bends down to be part of our singing,
a star is found in each chest,
and the wind bows to the pain of our voices.

—Hume Cronyn

Friendship

&

Love

My Friends

My friends
are ALL
afraid
I might change
and turn
into
a
child
or a monster.

My friends
don't really
like me
just my
bathroom
and only
if I have
shampoo, towels
& toilet paper!

My friends
expect me
to disappear
so I am learning
magic!

My friends
love me
if I
have
money
potato
chips and pop.

My friends
forget
my
birthday
they
forget I
have a
sense of humour
and a sense
of purpose!

My friends
forget I
am independent
forget I
have dreams
and a shadow
side.

My friends
forget I am
not perfect
and blame
me
for their unhappiness

so
are they
my friends?
Yet I love
them
otherwise
I would be
alone!

My friends
give
me
ulcers
give me
cheese and
chicken soup
from the
food bank.

So yeah
they are
my friends

and I
love
them
after all
they are my
friends.

—*Roberta Taylor*

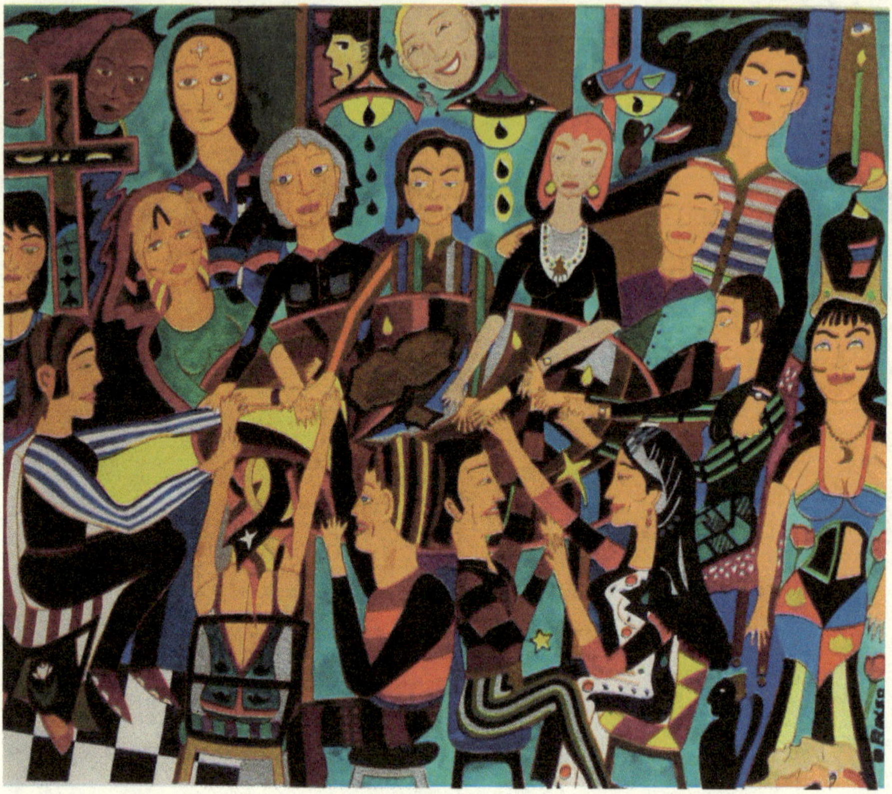

Don Baker

What to Win

It's an old, old life,
And what does it bring?
When I think that I know something,
Turn around I don't know anything,
Like an old, old tale,
And what does that tale say?
Tells me I'm an army soldier,
To the war I'll go away.

It's an old, old sun,
That shines down from the sky,
Sometimes think I've got the answers,
But the wind just blows me by,
Like an old, old dream,
That haunts me in the night,
Look around to find that something,
Find myself lost in the fight.

Heard an old, old joke,
And laughed the other day,
Guess I thought I'd heard it all,
But I fell down laughing anyway.
It's a balanced world,
And it's anybody's guess,
Most days sliding on bananas
Of tomorrow's wild distress.

There's an old, old song,
One that people love to hear,
In it the words say nothing's wrong,
That a friend is always near,
Like an old, old tree,
Rather planted in the ground,
Just want to stretch my branches free,
Hum like the wind and join that sound.

—*Don Baker*

Character Sketch

My sister
My soul mate
She who runs with the wolves

Her heart and mind
Her body older than mine
Long white hair done in a mullet

My sister
My soul mate
She who runs with the wolves

Her eyes are piercing to the soul
She is pleasantly plump
Her fingers
Long and dexterous

My sister
My soul mate
She who runs with the wolves

Priestess in her own Rite
A daughter of the Moonlight
She hears the cry of the moon's children

My sister
My soul mate
She who runs with the wolves

Sweet Medicine Woman's child
Her face crinkles when she smiles
Her eyes light up when she laughs

My sister
My soul mate
She who runs with the wolves

White Buffalo Woman's child
Her cats are her children
Nature the love of her life

My sister
My soul mate
She who runs with the wolves

She walks the moonlit path
She walks the red road
Always in harmony with each other

My sister
My soul mate
She who runs with the wolves

She is very giving and loving
Her friendship valued beyond treasure
A spirit akin to mine

My sister
My soul mate
She who runs with the wolves

Her hands are always busy
Doing this or making that
Dream catchers, Afghans and others

My sister
My soul mate
She who runs with the wolves

She writes of her children
The domesticated ones she lives with
The wild ones she runs with each moonlit eve

My sister
My soul mate
She runs with the wolves

Life is a journey we take with each step
Merry meet our paths have crossed
I wish her good journey and blessed be

My sister
My soul mate
She who runs with the wolves

—Brenda Swainson

Good Morning Sorrow

In a small room, under the roof of heaven,
I live in a pain and sorrow of loneliness.
Still I do not understand what has happened.
But I do understand her and am willing to give
forgiveness.

She is now with another man, in seventh heaven.
I live at the edge of hell, sick of loneliness.
Now I understand what has happened,
But I still love her and give my forgiveness.

Last night, I had a visitor, an angel from heaven.
He gave me strength, a hope in my loneliness,
But it was destiny what has happened
And I shall die without her, in my forgiveness.

—Aleksandar Korovljevic

IMOY

I remember . . .
The time when we would stand by the sink
you would wash and I would dry
What's a boy to do
with these memories of you?
And when I get close to another
my mind plays a vicious trick on me
and my hands still feel you
from many years ago
Although I refuse to cry
it seems I buried you long ago
so please don't get up dear
If I see you again
I could drag you home yet
new pet
but leave you
–on the pile
–in the corner
–under the coffee table
–under the sink
–beside the phone

Because I don't have a clue
what to do
with that stuff

–paper
–pens
–elastics
–cards
–envelopes

I feel the need to keep it
I don't know why but I know that
All I want is you

–Ken Cromie

Love Is a Slow Train

Love is a slow train
Going down the tracks
Between these sheets
Of snow and rain
Slow like the whispering wind
Low like a dirty word
In a restricted yard
By the bluest bird
On your ear in a dream
Tapping at the lips of invention

—Graeme T.K. Lawson

My Dear Love

The other day, I came across a word that I want to share with you. "Pearly." Pearly reminds me of you: of your beautiful jade face, your amethyst eyes, your ruby heart, your lapis lazuli ways.

It reminds me of your smile. Your gorgeous wide smile, so worry-free, showing off to the world those un-pearly teeth.

That your mouth is a healthy oyster where no pearl could ever grow.

That your mouth, too just and too worldly, too arid to cultivate pearls, is where only wisdom and love can grow to feed us all.

For as your teeth are now falling out to give way to little windows for the world to breath you in, I, as always, cherish your un-pearly teeth.

—Eugenia Cappellaro-Zavaleta

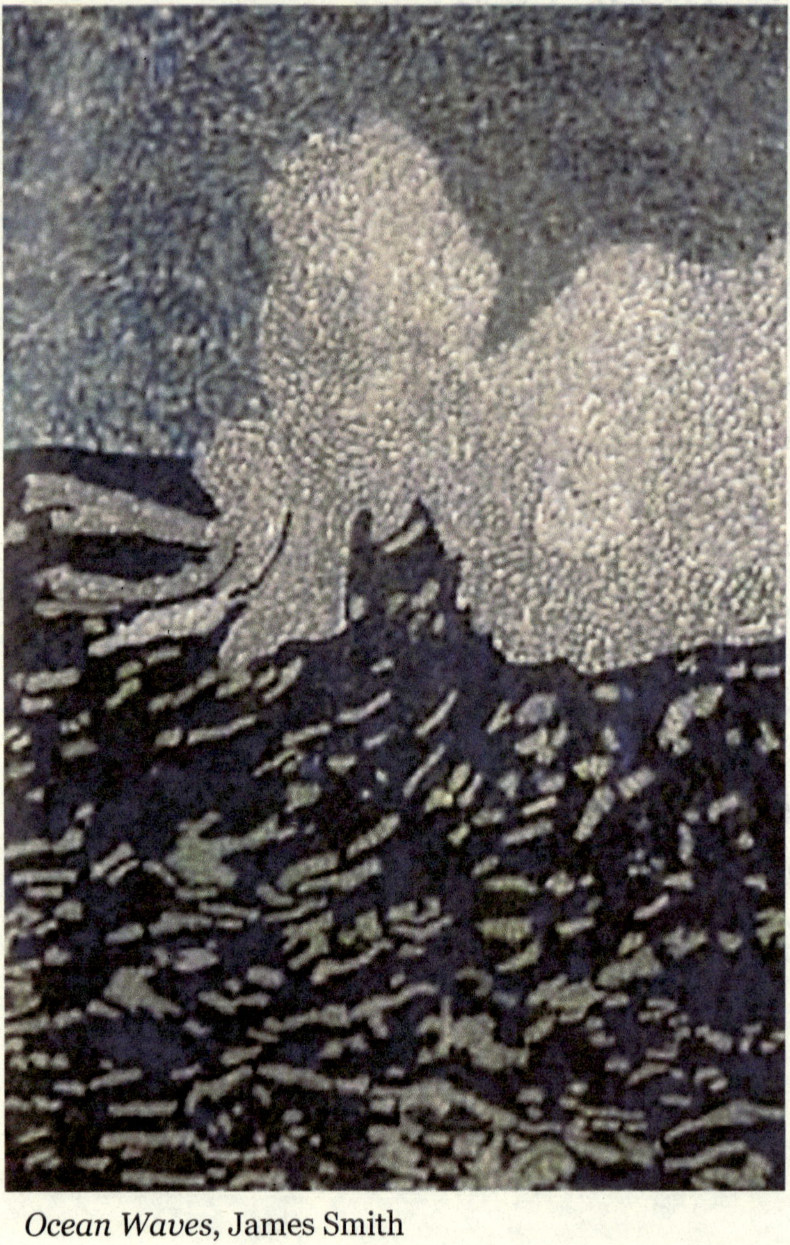

Ocean Waves, James Smith

something under semi-translucent leaves

once ...
someone — something
of earth born — but ocean bound

it was in a shady retreat
under semi-translucent leaves
I saw clouds fly over — white horses below
the sea awash — alight
and she so far — yet right there

I feared losing in her
lonely embrace
what — some moment of grace?
No
I simply feared losing her

but then
in a kind of storm
my thoughts
                    hush
                              like a field at dawn

the sky came raining down
and salt-specked gulls
perched on sun-beaten rocks
drank from the air
their outstretched wings
ablaze

                    the sky opened
                    and the vast night
                    collapsed into the sea
                    — we were solitary planets
                    in the deep

time
stood still

stood still

and the ocean
revealed its will

until
suddenly
a cracked smile — sympathy in brine
— mementos in the tide

now I chase echoes
counterpose words
to efface a lie

but the moment has died

— and this new one
                                        barren and drawn

—Chris Beyers

Two for Shannon

The old playground – there in the brush
and the ghosts   in the leaves

broken down a touch
and winter beginning to sing   in the trees

Shannon looks at me,
coming down the slide
with the wonder   in her greening eyes

I see my daughter standing and playing close by, leaning and making lots of noise   The expressions, now as she looks back at Dad and finds the drawer, opens it ...   She brings a ball to her mouth and gets up the stool batting with her arm and hand   Her delicate little hands apprehending things and the beautiful femininity of her touch   Up now on her feet at 8 ½ months   pulling at the ledges, the edges of our hearts

—Graeme T.K. Lawson

Notes

You and I left notes on the fridge.
Memory moored by magnets
Notes to remind us of paper bag lunches
And of assignments due
Notes as checklists to be tediously
Gone through before family vacations.
Each trip starting the same way, late.
Mom snapping her gum, not talking to you.

Then
Later
Too soon

Memories suspended in amber
Slipped away
on an unremarkable day
All your worlds flew away.

But the forgetting heart still loves
And we, your redacted, selfishly hope proximity
helps.

When I brought your shoes to the funeral home
There was a note in each one
This is a shoe.
It goes on the left foot.
This is a shoe.
It goes on the right.

—Shannon Quinn

Journey

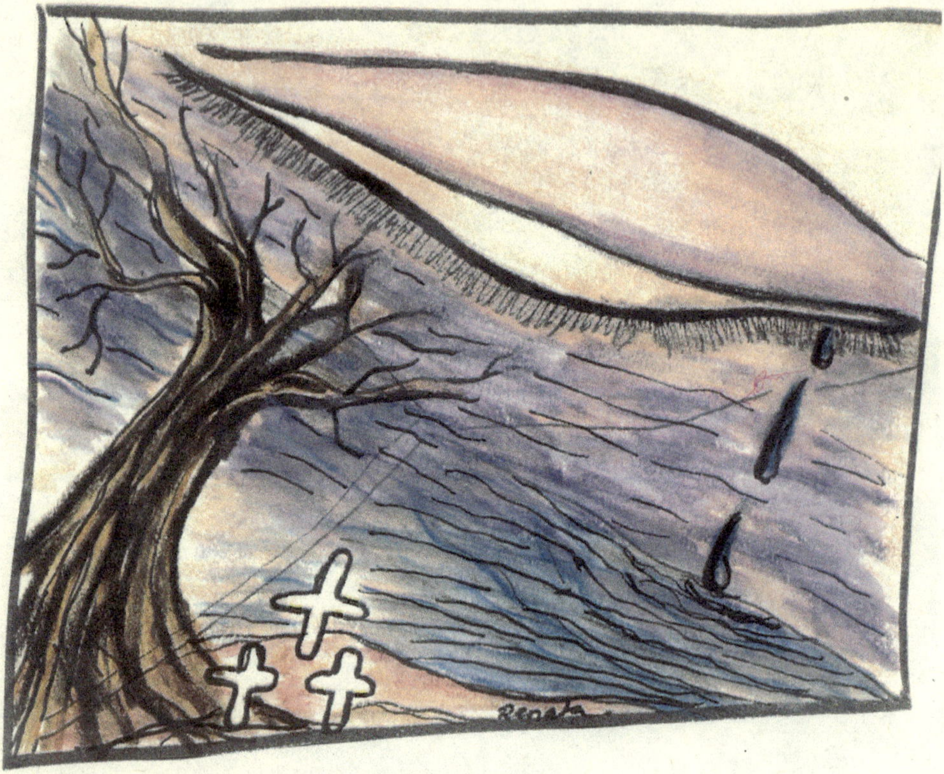

Dismal, Renata Edan

They Put Her Down in the Darkness

They put her down in the darkness. One lone owl hooted, disturbed by the sounds of dirt hitting her body. No one cried or prayed. In the morning there was no sign of this end, dismissal of life. The people went to church and touched hands, smiled beautiful smiles, not feeling the evil in their neighbours' hands.

Darkness again.

Something, or someone, is moving in the graveyard. In the moonlight it looks vague–girl, daughter, classmate reduced to spirit. She discovers finally that she has no boundaries. She learns to fly. She learns that in full daylight no one can see her. So she flies around looking for the men with the evil hands.

She's now nameless, always loveless, never finds the men. She forgets the sound of their voices on the wind. She had thought there was some kind of after-death club like Brownies or Girl Guides but maybe she can't find it (them) because she was wrong, or she wouldn't fit in.

She wonders about a word she'd heard once: "eternity". Is this it?

Still lonely, she learns to love what she'd been given...AGAIN. "Flying is beautiful," she thinks to herself. If only she could get the birds to see her, she can play. She plays with them anyway.

The men with the evil hands are never discovered.

–*Tyde*

Fire

The flame that had once been there was gone. A friend of mine had lost the spark in her eye and did not want to go on. The inner spark she once had, had been snuffed out. The fire that once made her feel warm and passive had gone deadly and spread through her body and her soul. The days when she would sit in front of her fireplace and daydream and all the passion she once knew had now diminished in her mind. Her soul had burst so badly from hurt and pain and great losses that her once light sparks of fire became a towering inferno burning out of control. It brought disaster and destruction with every passing day and night of her gloomy life. She could not again capture the old feelings of passion and warmth and beauty and romance. For in front of her all she felt was the hot roaring smoldering fire that made her feel nothing but anger, scared and empty.

You see her life became a living hell when her family perished in a fire. When they died, she had died along with them, and she felt she did not want to go on. She often asked the gods not to spare her, to let her body and soul go up in flames, like having fatal human combustion. For the fire inside of her body and mind was out of control and just kept burning her up inside, and she did not have the energy or the will to put it out, nor did she want to.

She would picture in her mind being a piece of wood, setting it on fire and watching it burn, and picture herself being that piece of wood, the bad stench of burnt flesh, the pain and hurt of sweltering skin. Knowing deep down inside that once the flames were out she would be at peace and in her heart she could rekindle all her feeling once again, because in her passing she once again was reunited with her loved ones. For after joining her loved ones, her candle that had once burned so brightly and sparked and glowed so brightly had once again come to life.

-Kathy Essery

RENOVATIONS

I was looking at some old buildings boarded up one day.

These buildings reminded me of how I'm under renovation.

At first I was surrounded by negative energy; things like hate, lust, greed, envy, etc.

Now I'm surrounded by positive energy; things like love, compassion, understanding, forgiveness, etc. I'm learning on my own how to overlook the negative energy and absorb the positive energy.

I'm still under renovation, because I still have some vices. I have found that tranquillity and meditation are good for the heart, body and soul.

—John Rogers

Returning Home

When I am old
I will not think of myself as old.
The definition of old
will have progressed into ancient.

I will have hair
the colour of moonlight
that captures every shade
of dreams
as they dance across
the waves of curls.

I will gather moments like jewels
and string them into stories
of histories and futures.

I will set myself at the centre of time
and weave possibilities
into a tapestry of life
that pleases both
creation and creator.

I will dance the morning awake:
softly
if my body
no longer contains
the ardour of youth,
but always
with as much passion
as my life
loves me to have.

I will be honest with myself.
The lies of self-protection
will have thinned to a veil
that can be shed as easily
as the tattered remnants
of the carefully crafted costume
worn by a movie castaway.

I will walk
in the path of my old dreams
crafting
a place for myself
in the realm of creative reality.

I will walk as quickly as I can
when my destiny is calling,
but I will stroll slowly and intently
chatting with people and birds and trees
when time allows.

I will embrace nature,
human and otherwise,
with a sense of wonder.
I will explore it
with as much innocence
as an overstuffed mind will allow.

I will not be so hard in judging others,
because I will know
that we are the same thing.

I will celebrate each sunrise,
and each sunset,
as though it were my last,
or the first of many,
on a journey towards myself.

I will celebrate each life
as though it were my own.
And each death as though
it were that of a good friend.

The world shall be my family
and I shall embrace it with love.

Thank the Gods
for being old,
or young,
or middle-aged,
or whatever it is I am today;
because
I have the opportunity
to express my will.

—*Raven*

Make Me a Promise

Make me a promise to never be lonely
And to find a new love and to be free as a breeze,
To go to a new land, a new home in the country
Away from the riffraff and tatter of these people.
Make me into a bird that can fly so far away from here
To somewhere so beautiful, warm and wonderful to stay,
Make me a dreamer.

Make me a promise not to leave them to die for no reason at all.
Make me a promise,
A promise to believe in all creatures, our Great Creator and Mother
Earth.
To listen to the wolf howling at the moon.
Keep me safe and warm.
Make me a promise to keep the land safe and free, to wander on my own,
To find me a teacher, to teach me a song
And to teach me about the trees.

Make me a promise to know how to howl loud and free.
Make me a creature to walk upon the earth
And run like a deer and swim like a dolphin. Make me a promise
To know my place in this time, in this future.
Make me a promise so things are well learned from one another.
Make me a promise to dance on the waters of the Sea and Ocean.
Make me the eagle that flies above the earth and protects its young ones.
Make me a promise of joy and laughter. Make me a promise of safety.

—Laughing White Eagle
Michelle Caron

prophesy

the dust was everywhere
the sand too, it was everywhere
between toes, under finger nails, in the corners
we were falling in and out of the night, dancing

the marketplace was full
the young women with laughing eyes
and it felt like we could laugh forever
like this summer evening would absolve us

> *the banished have returned*
> *the ancién regime has fallen*
> *and in this warm and expansive breeze*
> *incandescence, under the timeless night*
> *which reveals no record*
> *of what has transpired, here*
> *in memory's burned out fortress*

you know, there was spirit there
– much as talk of spirit is suspect, it filled us
and I felt that if the world were to end just then
we would have known something

I live for this once, if only to re-live
a loss – maybe of what has never quite been
except as an apprehension, or anticipation
of what could still come

tell me that you know what I speak
and that it was not for nothing
tell me that you saw what we were doing
when we forgot, for that instant

—*Chris Beyers*

The Beautiful Child

The beautiful child is now almost a man. I've been gone almost two-thirds of his life. So what right have I got to call myself mother?

She lay on the bed, twisted images slowly filtering through her awakening state. Exactly fifteen years before she'd been spread-eagle, heels pressing down hard into the metal stirrups of the birthing table. Head back, teeth clenched tight, while the emergency team of doctors yelled, "push". Through the haze of four epidural shots, pushing was the last thing on her mind. After the baby had been forcibly removed from her, just in time to save his life, there had been a few moments of calm. She was glad he'd lived, but that was also the moment when she realized she was not going to be able to do the job properly. The tears had slid down the sides of her face. It had taken five and a half years for her to admit defeat. Nothing about it was graceful, and she had hurt the child unnecessarily and deeply when she abandoned him. Regret was her only nourishment for many years. Long years of self-abuse. It had been her excuse for not living, because in her mind only a truly horrid person would not mother the lovely person he had turned out to be.

Things had changed. She was now on a journey to find herself before it was too late. Before there was nothing left to offer to the man he had become. She secretly wished for grandchildren to surround her heart with laughter. But in her advanced state of self-pity, it was hard to imagine him loving her enough to actually bring them to see her.

She reached over to the phone and dialled his number again – eleven long digits – and yet again no answer. The results of neglect backlashing on her. She cried. Sometimes, she thought she was just too old to start over. Then she stopped crying and tried again.

—Tyde

Bed

Dream factory
Symbol of my sobriety
Bed

Back meets bed
Unfettered plain where the emotional horse roams
Toss and turn a sea a port an idea a dream

This bed here now
A promise
One bed after another
Large bedpost marriage
A shallow grave for failed
Dreams of wedded bliss
Empty and fearful I could
Feel her body close between waking
And complete unconsciousness
Trying to hold on to that
But unreplaced
In a strange place
Bed

Small bed
Bunk bed
Forty men to a room
I slept in my shoes
And was strangely comforted
By that cocoon
Of shallow friends aplenty
And uneasy alliances

Up and out the goal
Single-stacked ownership of
Confined comfort
Every bunk a home
Like a ship at sea
Or a mine down deep

Luke, he was a cool hand
Lights out at ten, men
Bed

New bed
New frame picture of unknown
Family and future

Question mark
More of a good friend than an old friend
More of a holiday than a place of last resort
More of a comfort place than a plan of necessity
More of an expression than an obsession
BED.

—*Ken Cromie*

The Soul is Lost in a New York Minute

So this is New York?
I thought to myself
As we crawled ever closer
To a string of lights in the distance.

My lips had receded,
No longer smiling,
Pursed instead,
Immersed in thought as night
Threw its cloak down over the city
Tired from a long day of waiting.

I stared out the cab's window
No longer interested
Or perhaps just tired of trying to interpret
Broken English
Overlapped
With a store-bought Bronx accent.

I had come here
Trying to find
Memories
Or perhaps to create them
While the city still tried to forget –
September 11th still fresh in their pockets
Held there like a rich man
Clutching dimes
As he walks past a beggar.

The cabby looked back and mumbled something about
Ungrateful tourists.
I made a mental note of trying
To ease his burden with a healthy tip.

We began the slow crawl over the bridge
Nestled like spoons
In our concrete drawer.

My thoughts raced now, wondering
If it was indeed wise for me to come here.

On the sidewalk a girl lay in sleep
Not concerned about the noxious cocktail
That the cars dispersed
Like bartenders welcoming newcomers
To eternal damnation.

Then it hit me.

I had to get out
And go to her.

I yelled at the cabby who was unfazed
By my hysterical rantings.

Dodging cars I leapt onto the soft melting concrete.

Slowly I approached her,
Not wanting her to awaken, simply to watch.

She jumped up like a cat
Desperately trying to catch a string
Yet unaware that it has no claws.

"Get away," she hissed
And nestled up to the side of the bridge
Like a mother clutching a scared child.

"Here," I said not realizing that
I was handing her my wallet,
This leather portfolio that defines my status.
"Take it all."

"What?" she spat, looking very confused.

"I want you take this all in the hope that you can start a new life."

Still puzzled she grabbed the wallet and ran,
Yelling, "You must be crazy."

Then she was a matchstick engulfed in a sea of city lights that played like
fireflies in a dream of some past camping trip.

"Perhaps I am crazy?" I pondered.

But now I finally knew what it was like to be alone.
With no societal construct to guide me.
Away from cell phones and the meaningless pursuit of possessions.

I was free on this bridge.
As I lay myself on her dirty makeshift bed my heart rate slowed.

I had come to New York to lose a life like so many others.
To retreat to the shadows and become another pothole in the road of injustice.

This night, so pure, surrounded me and let me breathe away my soul.
The tears that fell
Were so pure and not a creation of some media sob story.
My last thought before sleep came:
Finally I am home.

—Tom Poray

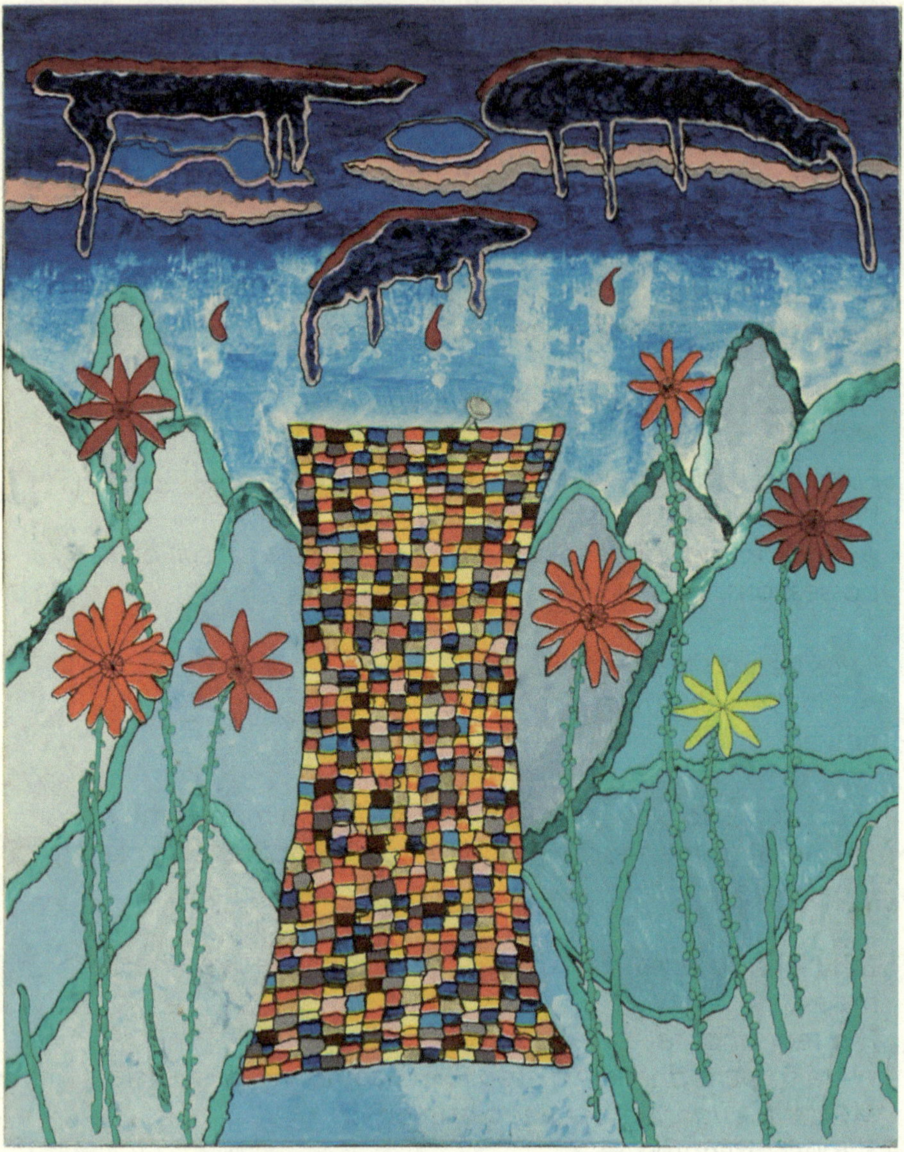

Tower of Tears, Tyde

A Letter (My Dear Soul)

I thought that you were lost or in hiding
I thought that you had abandoned me.
I found myself searching for you everywhere.
I looked in the trees.
I looked amongst the leaves
and the bark
and the roots.
I looked in the water
in the rivers and streams
amongst the fish
and abandoned tires.
I looked under rocks
amongst the dark, damp earth
amongst the bugs and worms.
I stood on top of mountains
and called for you.
I received no reply.
I only heard the sound of my own
Voice coming back to me
echoing in my ears.

I felt empty
I felt lonely
I felt sad
I felt lost without you
I thought that you had forgotten about me.
I thought that you had left me forever.
I couldn't understand what I had done wrong.

Why did you leave me?
Where did you go?
I placed ads in the paper
in the lost and found column.
Again, I waited for a reply
but nothing came.
Maybe my words didn't seem sincere enough.
Maybe I didn't say them clearly enough.
Or maybe you just didn't want to answer.
I felt like I had cried a million
tears
since you left.
I felt like my heart had splintered into a thousand tiny pieces.
I searched amongst the debris
looking for a clue
as to where you were
and then I sat
I sat with myself
in the quiet darkness
and I listened
I listened to the sound
of my own breathing
I listened to the sound
of my thoughts
running through my head
I listened to my tears
as they rolled down my cheeks
I listened
to the sound of my heart beating
I just listened

and listened some more
and there
in the silence
came a whisper
soft and low.
I knew it was you
and you told me that you had never left me
you were always here
you told me that you were waiting
waiting for me to be quiet
so that I could hear you.

—Renata Edan

Nothing Is Lost

This is for the inhabitants of unmapped prisons
For exiles of a country that never existed
For seething fundamentalists
And their teachers
For the bled
For the beggared
For thin ankles that totter in stilettos
For those that flicker in this world
never fully lit, always only almost
And especially for those who tried to know and love them.

Know that nothing is lost forever,
That threads from our bellies
link us in a human web
– an acrobat's net –
folding in on itself
revealing the disappeared, the dead, the awkward and the forgotten
who come to us as overwhelmingly skittish memories
bringing with them their phantom pain.

Know that in the floodplains of the heart
it is up to us
to tease away conditions that were set.
Erase accommodations made by time
as their ghosts surprise us,
the way the taste of salt on the lips
lingers hours after an ocean swim.

The papery flatness of the past will singe and curl in on itself,
leaving curious comfort in the safety
of how we know what we know
and how we forget.

—*Shannon Quinn*

Autobiographies

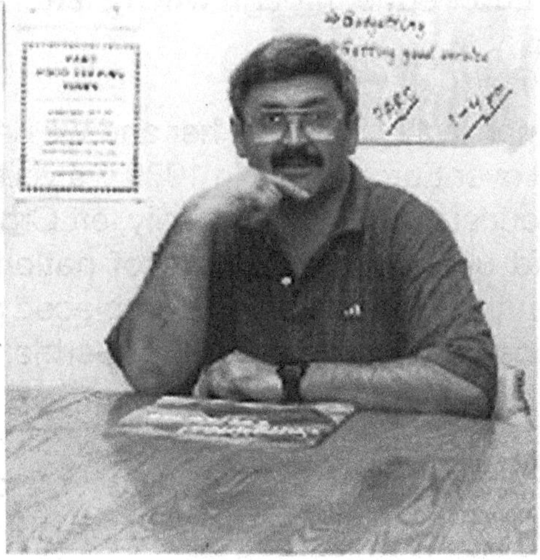

Aleksandar Korovljevic

I was born April 12, 1949, in the city of Osijek, the Republic of Croatia (formerly Yugoslavia), in a Jewish house full of antiques inherited by my late mother. My father, owner of several stores that sold fabric, later became the manager of the greatest fabric factory in town. He died when I was 17 years old, and this loss had a great impact on me. Because I was single (no brother or sister), I found consolation and protection in my mother who was a real lady, teaching me about gold, silver, gemstones, antique furniture, oil paintings, porcelain, etc.

I graduated from secondary school in my hometown. I also graduated from Law School in the nearby town of Novi Sad in the Republic of Serbia.

The English language I studied both in school and in university. I improved my knowledge through writing letters to a pen pal from California.

I married a woman in 1976. I loved her and we have two sons. We travelled all over Europe, and in 1980 we visited New York City, USA, as tourists. In 1991 my family left Croatia because of civil war and unjustified treatment of national minorities from Croatian authorities. We lived as displaced persons from the former Yugoslavia in the Republic of Serbia.

In 1993 I worked as an interpreter for UNPROFOR (United Nations Protection Force) in the war zone in Croatia (English and Hungarian). I survived an assassination attempt by Serb rebels.

In 1999 we survived a NATO air raid bombing of Yugoslavia, which lasted 78 days. In September 2000 we came to Canada, after which my wife decided to divorce me. She now lives with my two sons in Mississauga. I live alone in Toronto. My mother died in 2001. I am alone. I have only hope and the love from my children. I am desperate because I lost my dad when I needed him very much when I was seventeen. My son who is eighteen also needs his dad.

I express my thoughts and my feelings by writing poems and short stories, which are expressions of my inner life.

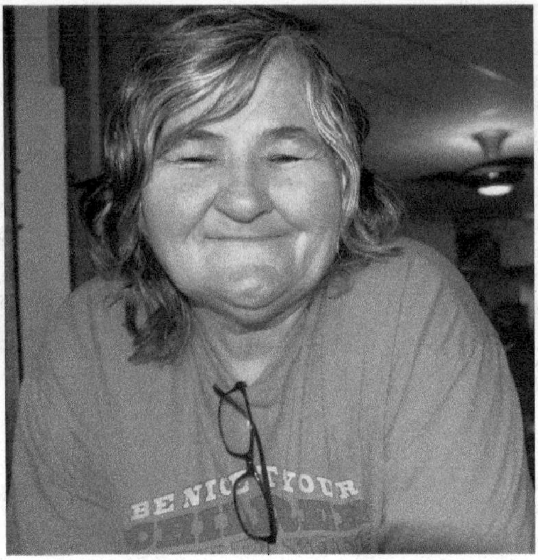

ALICE ROGERS

I am a writer. I've won three Bread and Roses prizes and Word on the Street, and I also wrote poetry for the newsletter that we have at PARC. Right now, I'm writing a kid's book called Manitou and the Three Huskies. I have three boys of my own. I have two cats, Nippi and Patches. My son lives with me for now. And I've been married for ten years. I've lived in Toronto since 1979. I'm an animal activist, and I'm into the Native movement.

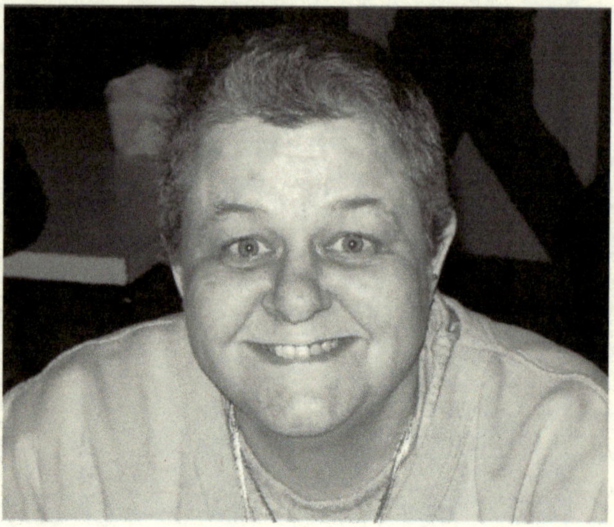

Ann Lapenna

I was born in Toronto and have lived here most my life.

When I turned ten, I moved to Feversham, Ontario and then a *few* years later moved to Ravana. I was in grade 9 and my dad took me out of school to work in the restaurant they owned. I like the city because there is more *freedom for* me; the country has its own advantages of fresh air.

Right now in my up-and-down depression life, I like to write poetry and study computers. I have taught computers at Parc and the New Hope Drop-In. I also like to make art and jewellery, both of which I sell.

I've experienced hardships, I've been close to death, but I've also seen the brighter sides of life. I have gone to hospitals, the Gerstein Centre and community drop-ins where I feel safe and able to talk to others when I need to. I have been abused since I was very young and now I am a survivor.

What makes me feel good is my dog, Scrappy – who is part schitzu and terrier mix – and doing my volunteer work with people with special needs at Bathurst Bowlerama.

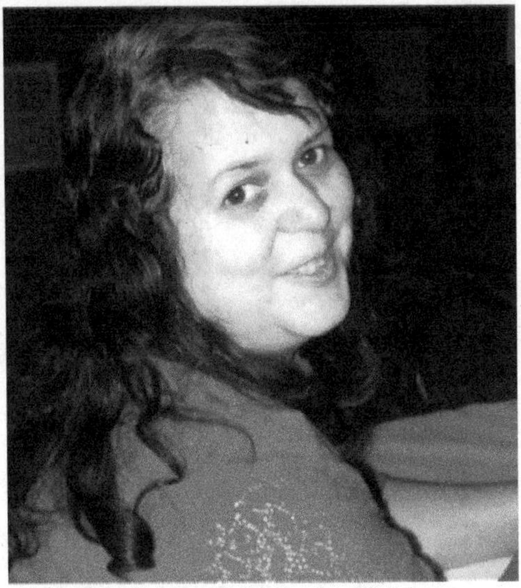

Bobbi Nahwegahbow

I was born in 1962 in Detroit, Michigan, and have an affiliation to the Birch Island reserve on Manitoulin Island. I'm an only child and I grew up in a large extended family. Due to my parents' early separation in my infancy, I was never raised directly by them. I grew up never knowing who I really was or where I belonged. I married at twenty-one and had a daughter. I am now a grandmother and am trying to keep these connections strong. However, it's hard when you've never had a maternal role model to parent effectively. I try to write out some of the demons I have through poetry and journaling, but my forte and main medium is poetry. I've been in Toronto for twenty-nine years and Parkdale has been my home for twelve. I love this neighbourhood and feel I fit in here. I also enjoy writing with other women and eventually would like to write with other survivors.

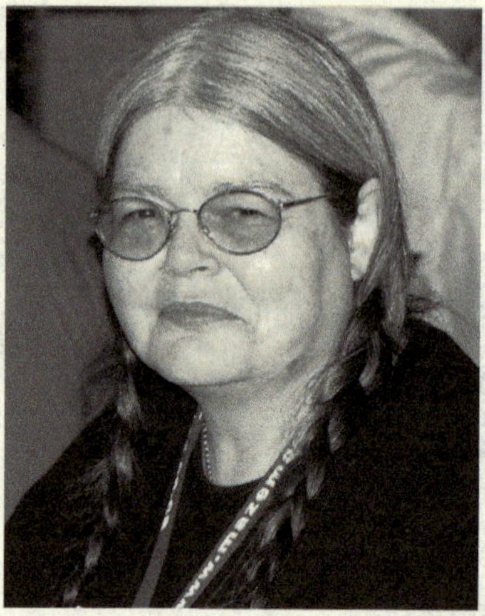

Brenda Swainson

I was born August 28, 1955 in Winnipeg, Man. I was/am a single mother of two children and a grandmother of three. I lived in Baker Lake (NWT), Winnipeg, Saskatoon, and the rest of my school life in Churchill. Churchill is Manitoba's northern grain port, situated on the Hudson's Bay and in the middle of the polar bear migration route.

My parents were born here in Canada but my grandparents are of European descent – Dutch, Icelandic and Norman. I have one younger brother and no biological sisters, though I am sister to many.

After a divorce in July of 1980, I moved to Toronto where I am currently living with my husband and two cats, Princess Chirpy and Purr Bucket.

A friend introduced me to PARC from about 1983 onwards, but I did not come by on any regular basis until 2002, not until my children were grown. Now I serve on the Board of Directors and on several committees at PARC.

I did become homeless in 1998 for a period of a month where I stayed in a shelter. I suffer from depression and osteoarthritis with a sleep disorder.

I wrote my first poem in the 1980's after being inspired by that wonderful book entitled 'The Lord of the Rings.'

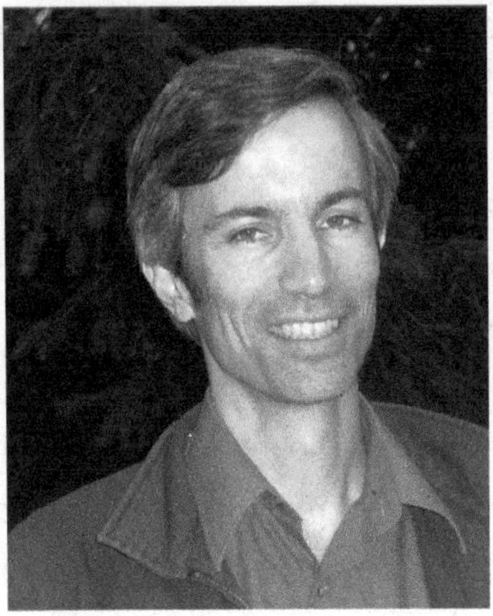

Chris Beyers

During a difficult time, I found myself searching. Sick of the books that had been distracting me, and tired of endlessly feeding thoughts into the computer, I was looking for something better to do with myself - a socially engaged job, with people. One day I took a walk into High Park, snow still on the ground, and sat for a moment under one of its picnic shelters, contemplating a pile of empty sleeping bags, blankets and cardboard before me. It wasn't long before a man and a television crew showed up and—after briefly acknowledging me—they started to discuss the anonymous pile in front of me. Masking my suspicion, I asked the man what they were up to. He explained that he worked with this organization called PARC, and that they were doing a documentary on homelessness in the city. After I learned his name and we conversed for a few moments, it occurred to me to ask if PARC happened to be hiring. Bob was somewhat taken aback, but considered the question for a moment. He responded that as a matter of fact they were hiring, and that he believed that coincidences sometimes happen for a reason. I could drop off my resume if I was interested.

The first person that I encountered at PARC was Melinda, whose genuinely open disposition towards myself as a newcomer immediately struck me. Later I was surprised when I was called in for an interview. I would leave there strangely inspired by the directness and originality of the people who I met. Soon I would be working on the floor, and drawn into the remarkable collage of stories that is PARC – stories such as those found in this book. And so, seemingly by no accident, I found my story intertwined with PARC.

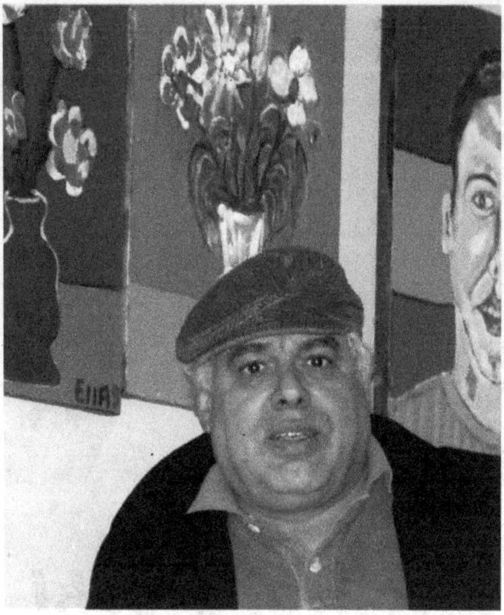

Elias Tabar

In my view we are living in a totalitarian society. We see variety, we have communities, yet we're segregated, labelled, stigmatized.

The war machine, the barbaric technological machine, has robbed us of our true selves and our ability to create a sane, humane society – why I sing and dance in the middle of all this controlled chaos is the reason of my being. My work reminds the world of what it has lost and/or what it's about to lose - wholeness and personhood.

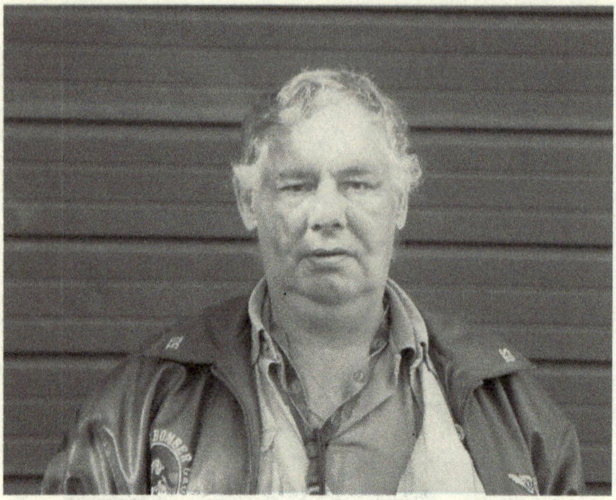

Eric Woligroski

When I was fifteen months old and when I was five years old, I was homosexually raped, probably the reason being to disorientate my normal life. I was preoccupied with filth all my life. It wouldn't leave my memory for a long time.

I started smoking marijuana when I was fifteen years old. What it did would only leave me paranoid. I first started drinking when I was ten years old.

I was using these defences to try to forget my problems. I had a lot of jobs since I was ten years old when I began working. I went to work at a lot of different jobs. What would I spend the money on? Basically, booze and drugs. I figured that if I worked hard I would forget about my homosexual rapes. I still could not forget the episodes.

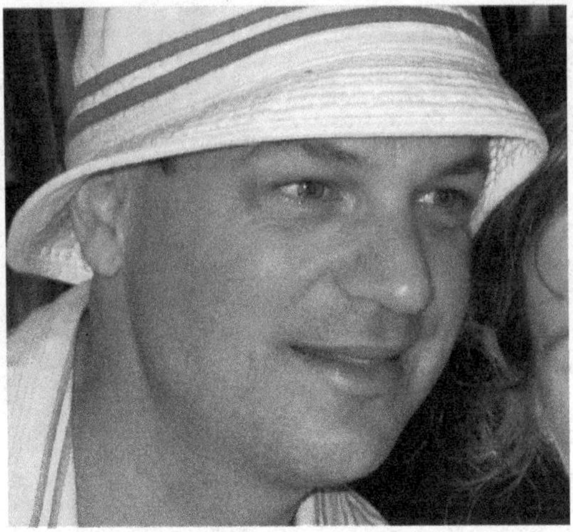

Graeme T.K. Lawson

I am forty years old. I was born in 1969 in Port Hope Ontario within Canada. My mother was 40 in that year. I didn't seem to like being born but I remember sliding down a hill with her on a toboggan and scarves in that city. I learned to speak and write French in an Immersion in Cobourg thanks to my parents. From there I went to Trinity College School where my Grandfather had been the Headmaster. Though he died before I was born, my father became the head of the English Department, and actually taught me there.

I began to experience difficulties with my thinking by the end of high school and was rebelling. But I joined a cultural exchange – CANADA WORLD YOUTH – and travelled to Brazil and to a town west of Quebec City – Donnaconna, where I worked on a small dairy farm. After that it was Montreal where I had deferred my acceptance to McGill University. I completed my Bachelor of Arts at Trent University in Peterborough in 1993.

I began writing poems near the end of high school. I would wake up in the night with words coming into my head that I felt compelled to write down. I was the mere vehicle for their expression. At that time I was loving to read 20th Century Poetry and Poetics (edited by Garry Geddes) which I had by my bed. The beats (Ginsberg et. al.) took my fancy.

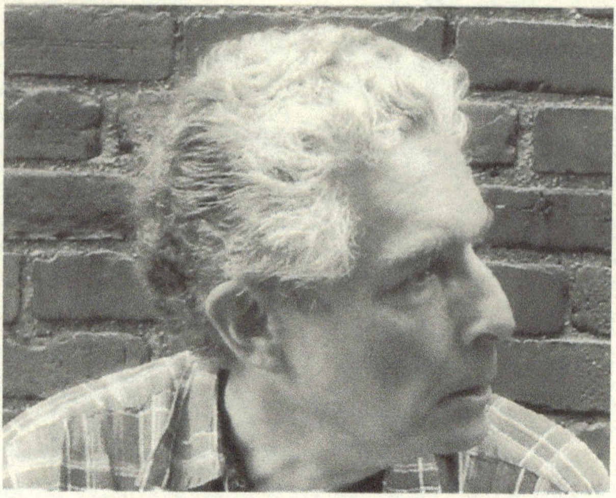

Guy Ewing

Guy Ewing is a community literacy worker who currently facilitates the Literacy Group at PARC. When he came to Poetry Night at PARC for the first time, several years ago, he fell in love with this monthly burst of words and music and has been a regular ever since.

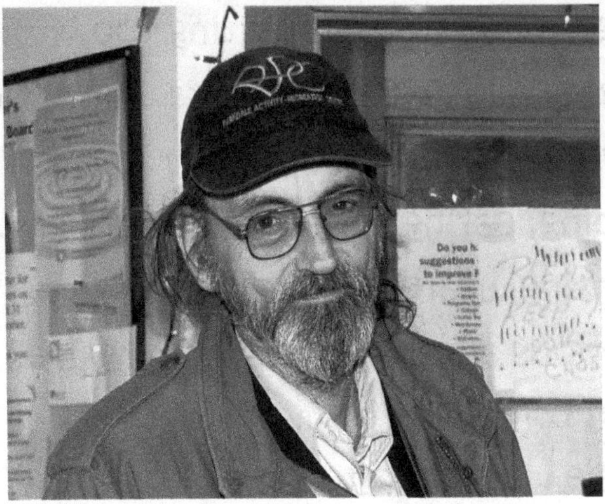

Heinz Klein

Let's be straight, ain't gonna wait,
being an artist is my fate.
Born and raised quite far from here,
with 'Humpapa' and lots of beer.
My mind's been bent, time by time,
but somehow I survived that fine.
In ragged clothes, peace was lost,
the streets my living, where I got tossed.
My art was all, all that was still me,
what helped me keep my sanity.
The need to help, and then to show,
a life which only reality would know.

My songs and words, my writing too,
my painting, writings, yes, that's what I do.
And acting, yes, well looking for what's right,
and helping, caring for all that is in sight.
Not wanting wealth, success and fame,
being serious about life that is my game.
I like you to be part of me,
to see the world and to get free.

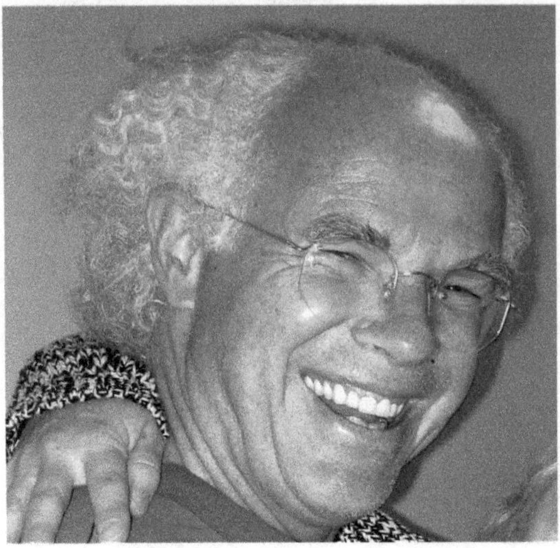

Hume Cronyn

I have been blessed with many names in my lifetime. At PARC alone, I have been called Hume, Humid, Humour, Humidor (when someone wants a smoke), Humes, Hues, Hubert, Humanoid (when someone wants to get my attention), Humewood, Chrome Human, Hewlitt, Huey, Hooley, Humus.

I'm always intrigued, tempered with a fair bit of skepticism, when someone says that their name means such & such in Greek, or Persian, or Sanskrit, etc. What do my various names mean? Obviously, a multitude of things.

For example, take my name Hume. One of the meanings is a hill. Not a lofty hill, like a mountain, but a gentle, stooping hill in the midst of everyday life, a hill from which I don't move at all. From a small height I want to watch everything that happens. How many years have I wanted to spend a week/a month/a year & say absolutely nothing. Like a hill, I would just watch everything that's going on around me. And then, there's that watching of what's going on inside. We don't spend enough time watching & listening to what's going on inside. Hills are famous for that. Everyone knows that. There's that famous Tibetan meditation exercise called the hill. I haven't been a hill for years, I must get back to my name.

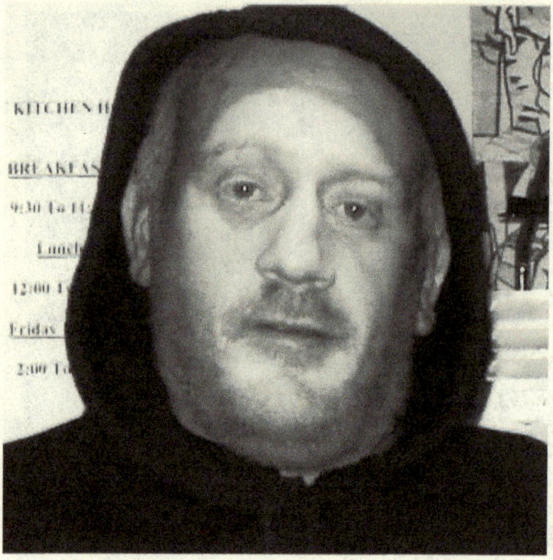

James Smith

When I looked out of the window of the Gray Coach, I thought back to when I was a child looking at the clouds. I see clouds as miracles in the sky with many shapes and volumes of white layers with blue shades of the atmosphere. I say to myself I like to paint pictures of clouds in the sky and I am an abstract painter that creates abstract illusion with colours. I just finished a piece with three sections: a water section, a sky section and an outer space section. With each section there is a lot of imagery within the art work, and when I look at the clouds there is a lot of imagery within the picture of the atmosphere. I also like the clouds that move across the sky for the reason that they change shape every few moments. It takes imagination or a good thought.

I was born in Toronto 34 years ago. I am a dedicated, hard-working person who can create beautiful artwork for people to look at. I have been at PARC for four years now and being on welfare while doing my work. A lot of people from PARC and around the neighbourhood like my work, but I am pretty well a loner. Life is art and I like to speak to people through my art.

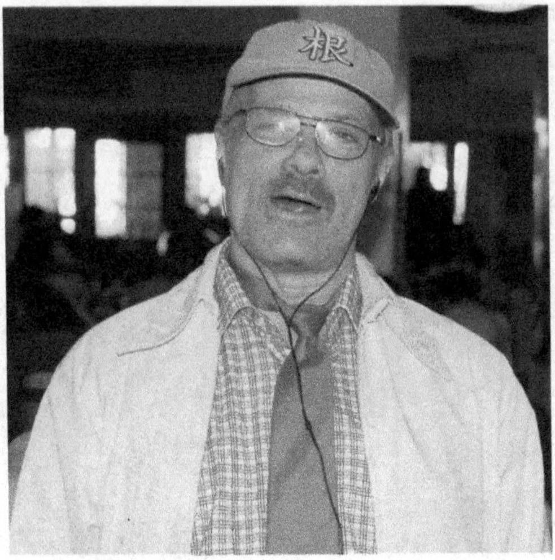

Jim Booth

Hi, my name is Jim Booth. I come from a family of 4 boys, 2 girls. My mother and father are dead. My life was not normal. I was a slow learner, but I made it through school. I had a mental problem. I thought I would never make it anywhere, but I did. I did odd jobs. Things were going good. Then I had a nervous breakdown. I ended up in the hospital. But I survived. I did O.T. (Occupational Therapy). Then I went to the workshop (Industrial Therapy). I then became an outpatient, but still worked at the hospital. I then started back to work doing gardening, shovelling snow, loading trucks, working on assembly lines. I sometimes worked a 60-hour week, other times 10 hours. I was a hard worker.

I started coming to PARC in 1983. I had fun. I met many people. Some have gone. I even was on PARC's board for 2 years. I went to writing workshop. I worked the coffee bar. Over the years I had a girlfriend who died in 1994. I dated her for 23 years. Over the years my memory is going so I can't work, but life goes on. I might be getting older but wiser. I hope I will live many more years.

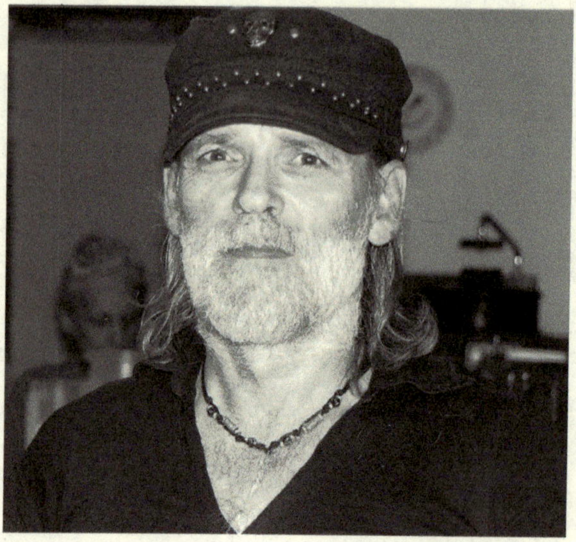

John Rogers

I was a shy, independent loner ever since I was six years old!

The other children used to make fun of me. My mother had told me that I was retarded. One of my teachers had told me that I'm like a sphinx because I would talk in riddles. Doctors had said that I'm autistic because I would build a wall around me to shut out the rest of the world and I had a hard time to open up to others.

My mother used to hit me with anything in her hands and would say that I should not have lived when I was born and I will grow up to be a nobody!

When I was ten years old I had to cook for myself and my sister, mow lawns, rake leaves, shovel snow, etc, to make some extra money so we can survive while our mother goes out getting drunk.

When I was twelve years old I told one of mother's boyfriends that he had no right to beat on us because he was not our father and I sent him to a hospital.

When I was thirteen years old, my mother had gotten drunk and had sex with me. After she was finished having sex with me she had said that she would have me castrated if I tell anyone so I ran away from home.

My sister and I were very close until she had married an asshole. He would beat on her until I had threatened to break his arms so my sister had told me to get out of their lives. They used to live on Kingston Road, but when I went to see them on Christmas of nineteen eighty-seven they had moved.

I have travelled around and worked on farms, lumber camps, forestries, freighters, factories and warehouses. I have slept in boxcars, snow banks, hostels, motels, hotels, jail cells, parks, abandoned vehicles, and houses. I'm maybe weak in the flesh, but strong in the spirit.

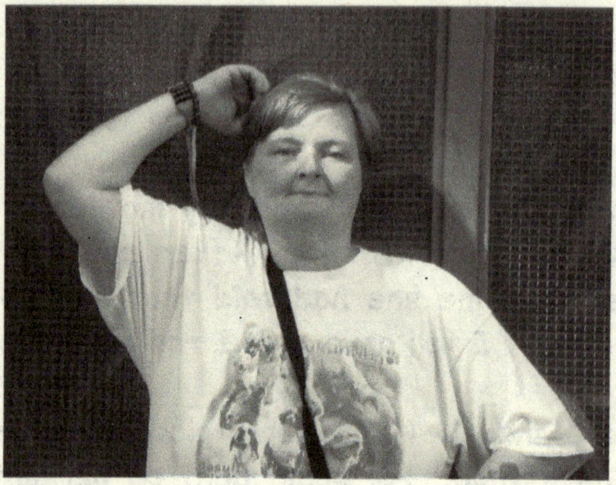

Kathy Essery

Kathalene, a passive Irish name.
Bright as the blue sky
Also green with envy.
The name sprang forward like the winds of spring.
For Kathalene has the strength of many mountains.
The more she falters down the more higher she climbs.
For the name Kathalene is like an armour. She is a protector of hearts and souls.
She is a protector of Herself.
For Kathalene is like the wind.
One day her air is soft and subtle,
Next day her air is harsh and hurtful.
For Kathalene is also like a bird flying endlessly in the sky,
Looking for somewhere to rest,
Looking for some place to call her own,
Looking for some kind of inner peace,

Looking for a place to rebuild her strength
So once more she can fly again.

For thc clothing of a name of Kathalene is far from bland,
For it is bold and beautiful and brings out the beauty in her.
The clothes do not swing or sway. They adjust to her curves and
movement
So she can move freely among herself and amongst everyone else.
For Kathalene enjoys freedom of movement.
She enjoys brightness and glamour and most of all just being herself
And being comfortable with herself.

For Kathalene being an Irish name is joyful, happy and a good luck
charm name.
For by having the name Kathalene I feel I've got a pot of gold at the
end
of my rainbow.
I feel there's no ocean I can't cross.
I feel that there's no mountain I can't climb.
I feel there's no such thing as the end of the world.
I feel there's no fear I can't cry.
I feel there's no place I'd rather be than here and now.
I feel there's no place like home.
I feel there's no joy like the joy of being loved by someone special
And I now feel that I have that joy.

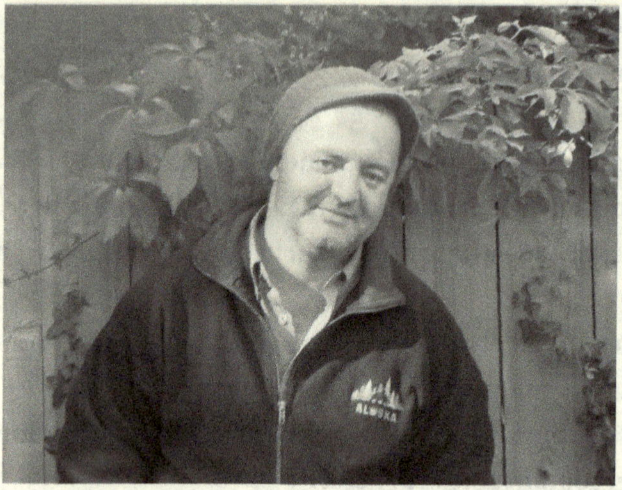

Ken Cromie

I was born close to Belfast, in Northern Ireland, August 14, 1969. My mother realized I had natural talent when I began whistling at the age of three. When we immigrated to Brampton, Ontario, I started studying piano and became interested in music. In 1986, I had difficulty in getting housing in Brampton and moved to Toronto. With Heinz Klein I formed a band called Bitter Sweet. I left Bitter Sweet in the fall of 1999 to pursue poetry ambitions and songwriting. I am currently building a studio called Glass Tree Sound. My screen name is Ken Nitrochrome. My favourite saying is: "False profundity is the flaw of reality."

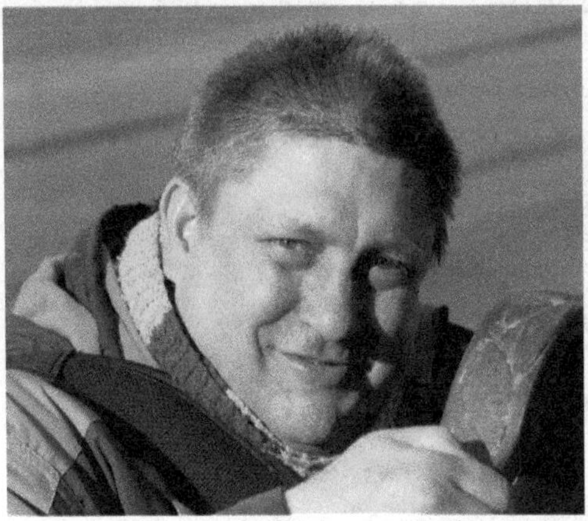

Ken Rosser

I was born into middle class circumstances, in a middle class neighbourhood, and went to middle class schools. After I left high school, I went on to college where I specialized in film, writing, photography and stuff. Lots of stuff.

As soon as I finished with college I quickly rose to poverty, drifting from job to job, and doctor to doctor, where I heard the refrain made familiar to me by parents, teachers, and friends, "Why don't you just act normal?"

Eventually, I ended up on disability, and from there, discovered PARC. I joined in on committees, and the writing group, and no one was expected to act "normal."

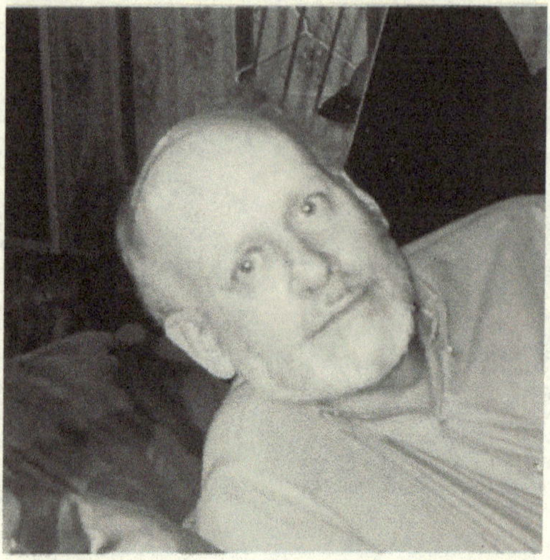

Kent Simard

He was just a waif of a man with blue eyes, grey hair and an olive complexion. He hoped to become a success at everything he did in life. He was bold, he joked a lot, he enjoyed painting the town, he stood up to jeers from others, he was a mean cat at times and wasn't afraid to give lip to strangers. He never found a mate in life. He ate well and that included eating fruit down to the rind. He enjoyed corn on the cob. He enjoyed to watch wildlife such as fox and deer but never toyed with wolves or grizzlies. There were few things he never became involved with, and that included riots. I guess that he was a bit vain but always remained on an even keel and seldom varied from that stance. He wants to buy a camper van and with a mate drive out west. He wants to use the scenery as a source of inspiration for his paintings. He feels that God gave him this gift to paint objects, scenes, or even things that come to his mind. That's me!

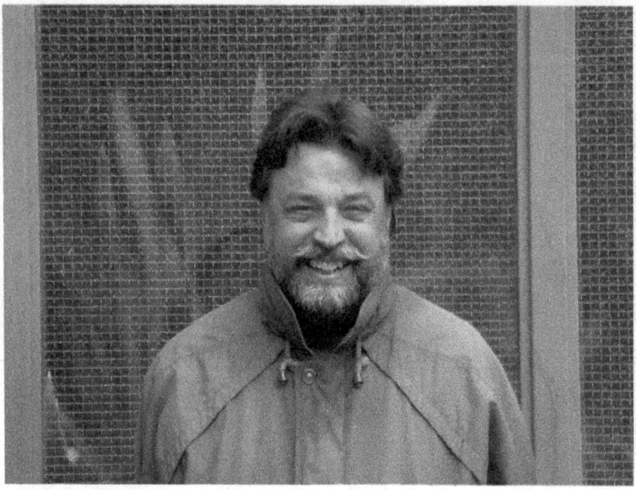

Luis Filipe

I was born in a middle class family in a small village in the heart of Mozambique. My father was an officer of the Portuguese Colonial Administration. I was a happy child and I had good teenage days. When I got sick back in 1985 with my delusions I had the time of my life. Then I crashed and, contrary to usual (people with my problem are alienated from their families), I was embraced by my family. I am very lucky today because Canada gave me everything I need. Thank you Canada and I hope that you will forgive me.

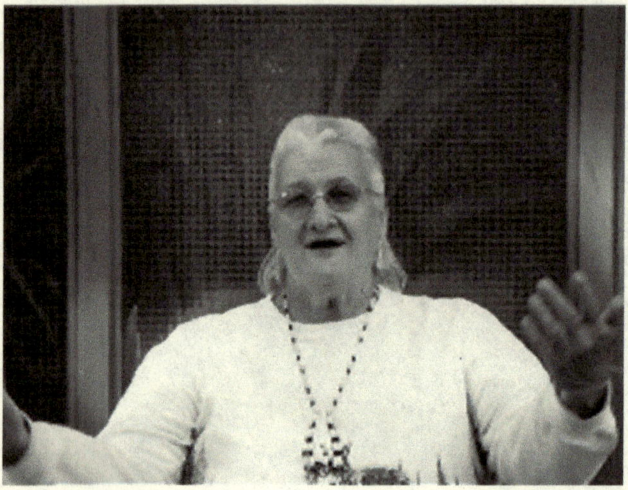

MICHELLE CARON

I have been here in Toronto since I was six months old. I had a good childhood when I was younger. I used to do a lot of running, swimming and just being myself.

I love nature. It has been my life, my whole life. I love farming, land, and my whole life as a child I've been not too far from my Spirit Animal, the Wolf. My native name is Laughing White Eagle. I am French Indian Metis and Cree.

I am a child of the Lord!

And my life has changed very much.

I had four boys and one girl. My children's names are: Robbie, Shilo, Gary, & Percy, & Evelyn.

This is my life, so I can't go any further.

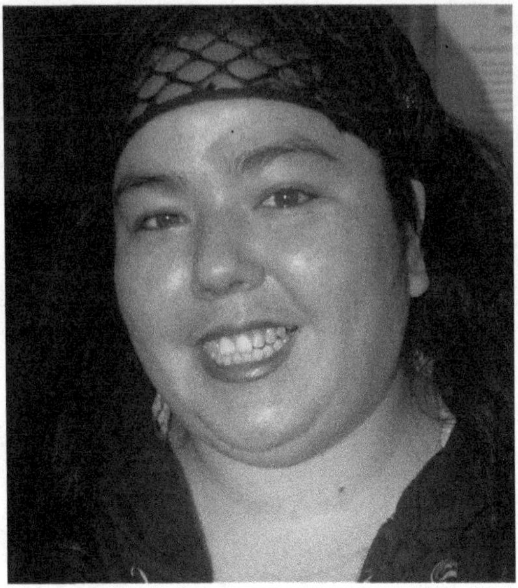

Ramona Mack

I was a teenager. I was a user. I was a drinker. My mom was a user and a drinker too. I loved my weed. It fixed my ways. I was a runaway teenager and my mom was a warrior and my ex-friends are losers and I was a second mother towards my sister and brother. They call me Mom. I was a cooker and my mom gave me some money toward our food.

I loved my mom and I love my brother and my sister. I loved my ex-boyfriends, but now I don't. My illness came. As I smoked weed I got worse than ever. I got sick. I thought it was a trick. I was ill and it made me want to die. Then I met Scott. He helped me out. Thanks to Scott I am better than ever. He is my husband and I am his wife. We both have the same illness and we go on with our lives.

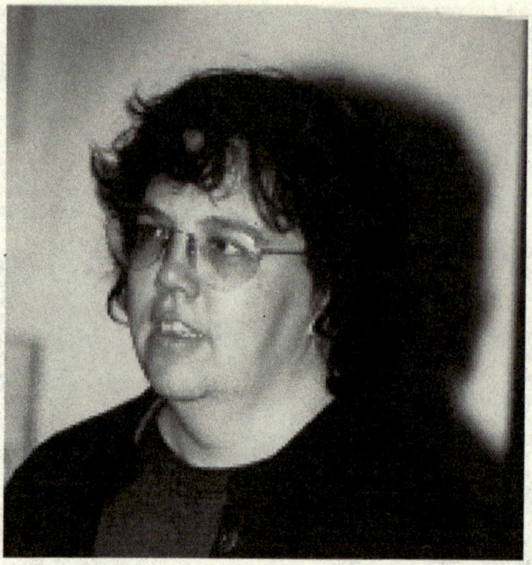

RAVEN

Born in 1959, I came screaming out of the womb after 36 hours of resistance and with the questionable help of a pair of forceps.

Raised by an alcoholic mother and a workaholic father, my sense of family and friendship came in the form of my brother Robert. Our common bond, surviving the insanity. His death in 1973 was probably the most devastating blow I could have ever received. And yet the need to take care of my mother through the ever-deepening darkness of her self-destruction that followed forced me to postpone my grief until I could be alone with it.

By the time I left home at twenty, the habit of suppressing emotions had become so ingrained that I had come to believe that I didn't have them anymore.

The next twenty years became a journey through the creative arts as I tried to paint, sketch, and tattoo my way back towards myself. In October of 1995, I wandered into a writers' open stage and was finally able to embrace the art that had always left me terrified. The page became my confidant, and sharing it with an audience became the hammer that helped to break down the wall of secrecy that had kept me from myself.

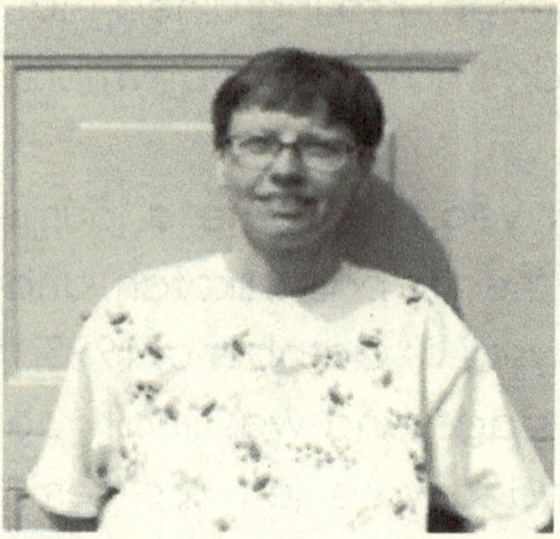

Renata Edan

My name is Renata Maxine Edan, but that is not the name I was given at birth. My birth name is Julie Ann Cotterell. I changed my name eleven years ago. Renata means reborn and Maxine means the maximum and Edan means fire. So my name means reborn maximum fire.

I was born in Toronto 46 years ago, where I grew up in Parkdale.

As a child I loved to sing, act, and draw. I have always been a creative person, and I hope that my writing shows that. At this point in my life my hobby is stained glass work.

I am presently back at school hoping to become a career and work counsellor.

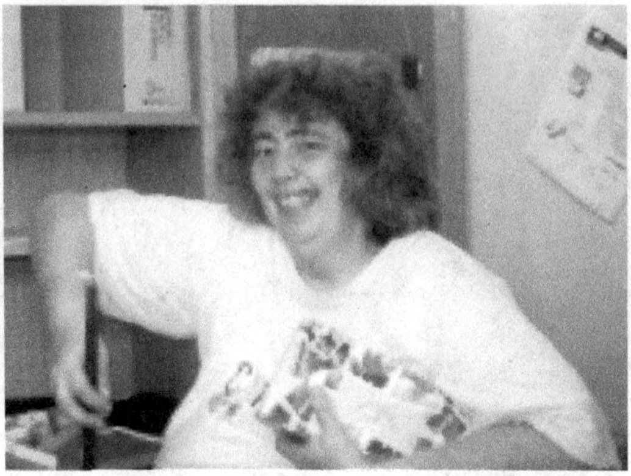

Roberta Taylor

Roberta is a poet, artist, and black & white photographer who has lived in Toronto since 2002. She's originally from Winnipeg and likes Toronto for its diverse culture. She loves cats, plays soccer at PARC, is a big fan of hockey night in Canada and wants to start a swimming group. She's been involved in professional theatre since she was eight. Roberta has lots of experience with spontaneous poetry and has introduced it to the PARC poetry night.

Guiding philosophy: there's always going to be days that you don't want to get out of bed, & other times when everything is perfect; and sometimes they occur on the same day.

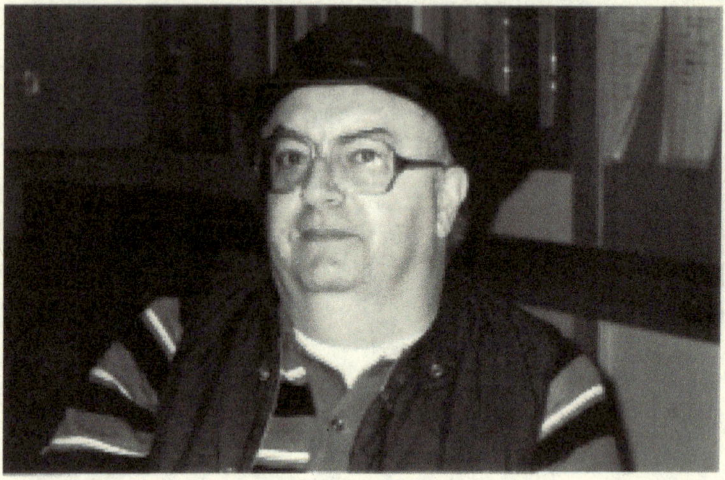

Ron Forestieri

I used to have a life or so I thought! In truth I have merely existed. When I look back on my life, at 56 years of age, I have little to show for it and consider my life a failure!

My parents moved to Canada when I was a year old so I have no memory of Italy. There were some happy moments in my childhood but mostly I remember neglect and abuse. Somewhere along the way I became emasculated. With my spirit broken I was unwilling to fight, so I was quickly targeted by bullies who made my school years a nightmare. I began avoiding my peers, preferring to play at home with my toy soldiers. Depression set in and became my common state of mind. By high school I was a social outcast. I have never married as relationships were few and brief.

When I started working I was continuously intimidated and overworked until I started having mental breakdowns. I desperately tried to salvage my life by seeking therapy but it didn't help! Repeated burnouts eventually cost me a 20-year computer career.

What had kept me going over the years was my love for horses and roller skating. Riding horses has always helped me to unwind when I am stressed. As a teenager I became a regular at the Terrace where I learned to waltz on roller skates. Waltzing became the greatest passion of my life and through this I met my one true love. It was the only time in my life that I was genuinely happy. A jealous friend used lies to destroy that relationship. No one has ever been able to take her place in my heart.

The anguish of a broken heart is painful to live with so I became involved in hockey. Fishing trips brought back happier memories such as catching my very first fish in Grenadier Pond. I joined bowling leagues, winning several trophies and one tournament.

In 1988 I became a bus driver. Bullied and overworked again, I developed diabetes in 1994. One year later I was injured on the job and was promptly fired without severance. All efforts to obtain my severance pay failed. My therapist determined that I was too burnt out to ever work again, so I was placed on Ontario Disability (O.D.S.P.). In 1996, despairing and broke, with little hope of recovery, I moved into Parkdale to wait for death!

The most redeeming statistic of my life is that I enjoy helping others. I have served as a Big Brother four times and coached boys' hockey. In 1999 I began volunteering at PARC where I run a computer program, obtain donations for the centre and plan outings for the members. For a year I was a writer for PARC's monthly publication. In 2003 I became a volunteer sportswriter for a women's hockey league. Lately I've been helping out at ReBoot Canada. I have found new hope through helping others!

The best way to describe myself now is that I am a malcontent living in a time that I am not compatible with. I personally believe that children are the world's most precious resource, but too many people value arrogance and greed above all else. The state of the world supports my theory! As a malcontent I dream of a world where no child is ever hungry or abused. It is the world I wish had grown up in!

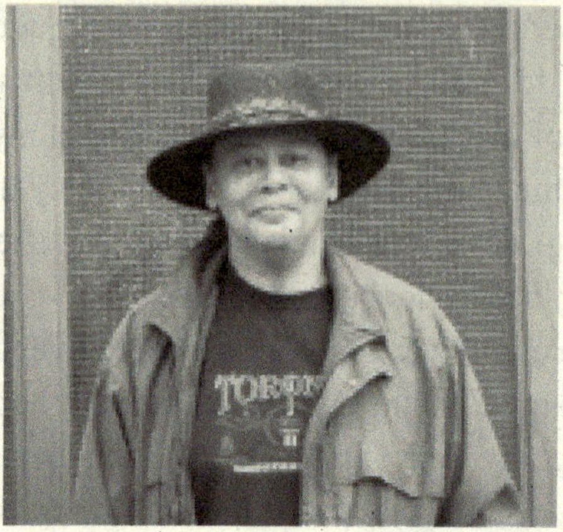

Terence Eustace Williams

I was born in Cape Town, South Africa on November 28, 1950.

I moved with my family to the United Kingdom in January of 1951. We then moved to Canada on June 15, 1959. Things went awfully wrong for me in the fall of 1985 and early in 1986. I found myself in and out of the hospital system suffering from mental health problems. This cycle went on from 1986 to the year 2000. By the year 2001 life was returning to some normality. During the years of 1986 to 2001, I had been terribly isolated here in the city of Toronto. I became a member of Parkdale Activity-Recreation Centre and my isolation was starting to come to an end. I have been a member of Parc for the last five years. I now serve on the Board of Directors and I'm starting my second three-year term. I sit on several different subcommittees of the board including the governance committee, executive committee, and several more.

I have been very involved with recovery for psychiatric survivors including my own recovery. I'm involved in the Ontario Recovery Campaign in Toronto and throughout the province of Ontario. I need to speak of the isolation that those of us in the mental health system suffer from and must endure. I want to reach out to the broader community to tell my story and how isolation affects the lives of survivors. Some day I would like to form a group that would be involved in public relations here in the Parkdale community and in Toronto as a whole. This group would educate the public about the oppression and discrimination and the stigma that people who have been labelled with psychiatric illness face in their everyday lives.

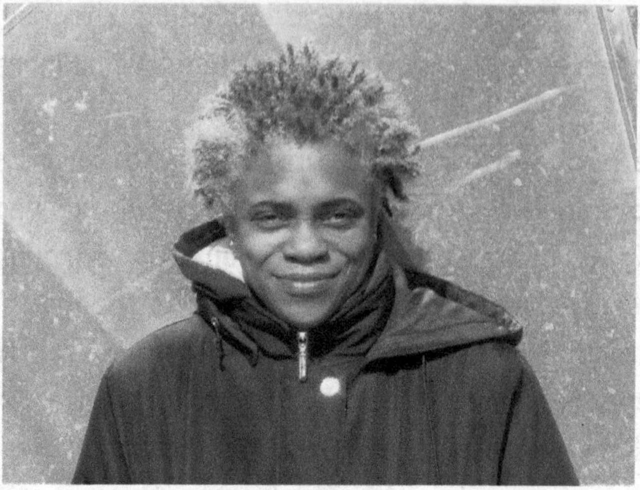

TYDE

Tyde is a
brown-skinned
visual artist
impro-blues singer
comedian
writer
mom
social activist
volunteer
chronic pain sufferer

who lives her life fully
and with

Great Joy

Acknowledgments

We would first like to thank all of the contributors for their patience in the long process of this book's publication.

Thanks to Calla Haynes for her photographs of the writers, Corey Mihailiuk for his photograph of the David Morriseau painting, and especially to David Bebee for taking the rest of the photographs of the artwork.

Finally, we are grateful to Alice Rogers, Tyde, Ann Lapenna, Tracy Cocks and Guy Ewing for reading and commenting on earlier versions of the book.